You Can Read a Face Like a Book

How reading faces helps you succeed in business and relationships

BY

Naomi R. Tickle

You Can Read a Face Like a Book

How reading faces helps you succeed in business and relationships

By Naomi Tickle

Design, production and editing by Strange View Marketing & Advertising

Sketches by Alex Tickle and Susan Cranbourne

Published in the United States of America

By Daniels Publishing

Naomi@thefacereader.com

First Edition: August 2003

ISBN 0-9646398-2-3

$14.95

YOU CAN READ A FACE LIKE A BOOK

TABLE OF CONTENTS

ACKNOWLEDGEMENTS

I would like to thank the many people who agreed to be interviewed for this book. Their stories have given my book a deeper level of understanding about the strengths and challenges within us all. Their contributions are greatly appreciated.

I express my thanks to the late Edward Jones and the late Robert Whiteside, who laid the foundation for this work. To all who have followed in their footsteps for their contribution to furthering the studies of physiognomy.

I would like to make a special acknowledgement to Norma Strange and Lisa Hewitt for taking this book from a concept to a reality. Their support for this project is greatly appreciated.

Special thanks to my husband Andrew; he was always there for me, patiently listening to my constant chatter on my latest insights and supporting me during my moments of self-doubt. This book would not have been possible without him. To my children – Martin, Jane, Antony and Susan – who have always supported and encouraged me in my work, even when they have heard me talk about the same traits a thousand times. I feel very fortunate to have such an incredible family.

Thank you to the many students and friends who have shared their enthusiasm and support for this work. A special "thank you" to Dorit Oren, Krystyna Foster, Susan Pryke, Michael Gilbert, Chip Carpenter and Jenny Fall. Thank you for all your help, inspirational ideas and referrals. I shall be forever grateful.

To the readers of this book, thank you for your curiosity to learn more about yourself and the people you meet. The difference you can make in this world is to share your newly acquired knowledge with others. The idea is not to use face reading to judge people, but to understand and recognize that we are all unique individuals. We all have strengths and challenges. It's how we choose to master them that will make the difference.

FOREWORD

It would be true to say that knowledge is power, in fact in what has oft been called the information age it is actual currency. This is the main reason why I spend thousands of dollars a year on books and tapes and videos that offer me knowledge. I have read everything from Nietzsche to Goethe, Blake to the Bible. Why do I do it? Because I am hungry for information and every book I read empowers me; it is an investment – one of the best I could hope to make – in me.

I pride myself on being able to choose the right information, to grow my mind and that is why I am delighted – nay, honored – to pen a few words for the introduction of my friend Naomi Tickle's latest book. Delighted because I get to read it before it hits the presses and the best-seller stands, and honored because the information it contains is extremely valuable in so many ways.

This book is filled with knowledge of the most important nature: it is about you, and the more you can know about yourself – how you tick, your challenges and strengths – the more you can shape your future into the positive projections that you see in your best mind's eye.

I first spoke with Naomi when she did a face reading for me from a photograph. Actually, she changed my friend's life with one reading. He recommended her to me. I was very intrigued. When I rang Naomi in America for more detail on face reading she was out, so I left a message. To be honest, I didn't really expect her to get back to me. Most people, particularly if they are well-known authors, never get back to you, especially long distance. I was delighted the next day when Naomi did get back to me, and not only was she was gracious, charming and patient, but she was also extremely generous with her time.

She didn't know me. To her, there was no immediate profit in me (there's an old saying that you should never judge anyone, but if you do, judge them on how they treat people who are of no profit to them). If I brought a book from her it probably would not have even covered the bill for the call. She even offered to give me a free reading from a photograph. That's why I knew she was good, and what she had to offer was important. And when Naomi did my face reading, I am delighted to tell you that it was (scarily) accurate. I was amazed at how much she could tell about me without even having to meet me in person. The information she read from my face substantiated my strong points, about things that I needed to trust more, and helped me to isolate parts of me that still needed work. The reading gave me a positive sense of direction and really helped me to let go of things that were no longer producing for me. I was delighted. In that one reading I learned a little bit more about myself, and that, enabled me to go a bit further along my journey.

One thing I have learned is that we are an inspired species, endowed with the magical ability to create. We can have anything, be anything, and go anywhere. We are all given numerous gifts when we land on this spinning planet. Once we learn to apply them – once we learn how the controls operate – the skies are not the limit. They are just the first stop in a universal journey that is both exciting and attainable.

This is a wonderful and innovative book by a gifted, generous writer; it will help get you there (wherever your there is). I whole-heartedly recommend it to those with their feet on the ground and their eye on the stars.

Geoff Thompson
Coventry, England

INTRODUCTION

Since the time of Aristotle, scientists and philosophers have been fascinated by the relationship between an individual's physical features and their personality traits – between one's physical structure and one's behavior. Physiognomy, the study of the face, is about 2,700 years old. It has intrigued and puzzled scientists for years. The first known face readings were made by the Chinese, they used them for diagnosing medical conditions. Later, the structural indicators of the face were used for determining personality types this also included predicting a time frame in a person's life when they would reach their greatest potential.

Scholars from Europe also subscribed to physiognomy (pronounced "fis ee ah nuh me"). These observations are mentioned in the Jewish "Cabala." Shakespeare, Milton, Dryden and many of their philosophical followers made popular use of physiognomic theory and principles. Toward the end of the eighteenth century, Johann Kaspar Lavater – an Austrian pastor, teacher, poet and artist – undertook the exhaustive task of classifying facial features along with mental abilities and predispositions. His Essays in Physiognomy became a major resource in the field and he became known as the discoverer of this new science.

In the early part of the nineteenth century, Franz Joseph Gall proposed the theory that the shape and contour of the skull also indicated that certain areas of the brain were particularly strong or influential. He identified 27 prominences of the skull that reflected attitudes or behavior of the individual. His observations were drawn from a more substantial base than that of those who preceded him. Johann Gaspar Spurzheim systematized and further researched Gall's work and introduced the term "phrenology" – the study of lumps and bumps of the head which was very popular in the nineteenth century. Spurzheim lectured throughout Europe and the United States in the late 1800s and early 1900s. Later, the phrenology banner was taken up by the Fowler brothers, who turned it into a sideshow and a commercial enterprise. Eventually phrenology lost credibility and fell into disrepute.

In the 1940s and 1950s, William Sheldon, a psychologist, studied the relationship between body build and personality. He suggested there were three basic body types, which he called "somatotypes." His theory met with the same fate as phrenology, although it is still promoted today in many of the self-help books. Despite the frequent departures from the course of investigation of human behavior, the idea that there is some sort of genetic connection between physical features and behavior remained alive.

Several others have attempted over the years to revive the idea of physical-features typing and to renew the search for provable relationships between features and personality traits. In the 1930s, Los Angeles judge Edward Jones observed the behavioral patterns of the people who appeared before him in court. He became so fascinated by his observations that he dropped his judicial work and researched the field using works that were published by Lavater and other notable authors on the subject. Using established scientific principles, Jones looked at 200 different facial

A PSYCHOLOGIST APPROACHED ME SEVERAL TIMES AT AN EVENT. WITH SOME RELUCTANCE, HE AGREED TO A BRIEF READING. WITHIN THE FIRST FEW MINUTES, I WAS ABLE TO DETERMINE HE SUFFERED FROM EXTREME MOOD SWINGS. HE WAS AMAZED THAT I HAD UNCOVERED IN JUST A FEW MINUTES WHAT HAD TAKEN MONTHS TO DISCOVER BY A PSYCHOTHERAPIST.

YOU CAN READ A FACE LIKE A BOOK

features and later narrowed the number down to 68. His studies included the hands and body proportions. His research had ninety-two percent accuracy for personality profiling. His system replaced many of the older methods for "typing" people. Thanks to Judge Jones, the "new" physiognomy became the modern-day scientific approach to reading faces.

Fascinated by the differences between one side of a person's face and the other, Jones concluded that numerous differences indicated extreme mood changes. When there are nine or more significant differences, the individual will experience more mood changes than those individuals with more symmetry. Often, individuals with these mood changes are perplexed by them.

Jones' contribution to the understanding of human nature, as it is revealed in the face, took physiognomy to a new level of acceptance, credibility, understanding and application. He applied the new physiognomy for jury selection, personal development, improving relationships, understanding children, sales and for career assessments.

In addition to the practical uses of face reading, further studies were conducted in San Quentin Prison during the 1940s. Warden Clinton Duffy stated at the time, "Many of our men here have been helped immeasurably by your staff. It is my hope that in the future we can broaden the scope of this great work." George H. Cantrell noted, "As a psychologist, having spent many years in vocational counseling, we now accomplish in hours better results than we would in days before practicing the principles taught by Jones and his staff." In 1943, a study was conducted on the freshman class of the United States Air Force Academy to determine how many men would stay the course. The study predicted outcomes with 96 percent accuracy.

Later, Jones met up with newspaper editor Robert Whiteside who was – like many before him – somewhat skeptical. However, once Whiteside received a consultation he quickly converted to becoming an ardent student and advocate of physiognomy. In the 1950s and 1960s Whiteside conducted further research on 1,028 study participants to determine the accuracy for personality profiling, relationships and career assessments. He and his colleagues found physiognomy to be 92 percent accurate for personality profiling; 86 percent of the study participants stated the information helped them in their relationships; and, for career assessments, 88 percent stated they were satisfied with the job recommended to them.

In his research, Whiteside observed that the features on the lower right side of the face from the base of the chin to the eyebrow were inherited from the father. The features on the lower left side of the face come from the mother. In contrast, the upper left features were inherited from the father and the upper right features the mother. If the parents had very different features, the child may inherit both.

Whiteside's findings helped to explain the significant mood swings that many people experience. Noticeable differences also pointed to incompatibilities between an individual's mother and father. As one couple told me, if they had only known this before getting married, it would have helped them get through the rough spots...or they would even have reconsidered the relationship.

Since Whiteside's time, these observations have been validated by thousands of people who have received personality and career profiles. Many of my own clients have stated they have either entered in the career selected for them, signed up for a course on the subject, or confirmed that it had been their childhood dream. This was the case for a 74-year-old woman who came in for a consultation. When her traits were entered into the computer career-matching program, the analysis indicated she should have been a pilot. Apparently that was her dream as a teenager. Instead, she got married, raised a family and left her dream behind. I had no prior knowledge about her dream. No questions had been asked. The information gathered was based strictly on her physical features.

Some psychologists think physiognomy is "New Age voodoo." Not so long ago, anyone suggesting that there was a connection between one's physical features and one's behavior or personality predispositions might have been considered crazy or possessed – put into prison or, worse still, burned at the stake. But science has provided some credibility for this "voodoo," much like it has done for other ideas that were once considered "weird" and "bizarre" – like the earth being round and the earth revolving around the sun.

From a physiognomist's viewpoint, tendencies are genetically inherited from our parents, however, the home environment and personal circumstances can be major influences that heighten or modify these tendencies. This goes for the positive traits as well as the negative ones.

If you were to look at the photographs of your ancestors – and knew what to look for – you would be able to see which traits you had inherited from various sides of your family. After reading this book, you should be able to do this.

SOME YEARS AGO, I RECEIVED A REQUEST TO DO A READING OF AN OLD PHOTOGRAPH OF A GREAT-GRANDPARENT OF A CLIENT. THE CLIENT WANTED THE READING TO BE AUDIO TAPED, WHICH WE DID. SUBSEQUENTLY, THE TAPE WAS PLAYED AT A FAMILY REUNION. DURING THE PLAYING OF THE TAPE OF MY READING A YOUNG BOY – A DESCENDANT OF THE PERSON IN THE PHOTO – SAID ALOUD, "MOM, SHE'S DESCRIBING ME!"

After you have read this book, line up some old family photographs and look for some of the similarities in the faces. Start at the top of the head and work downward. Their personality traits will begin to unfold.

If an individual inherits a number of opposing personality traits, he or she can experience huge mood changes. The person will be on Cloud Nine one moment, then slide "down into the dumps" in the next. There is no rhyme or reason – the person is actually perplexed by their unpredictable behavior. When I first discovered this about myself during an initial consultation, the "light switch went on." Suddenly, mood changes began to make sense. Those of you who experience them will be glad to know there are ways to work through them.

Take a look at United States President George W. Bush. You will notice that the inside corner of one eye is closer to the center of his nose than the other. For the most part, he will be fairly tolerant; then, out of nowhere, he will have an outburst. This is a sign of having both tendencies – his mother's wide-set eyes (High Tolerance) and father's close-set eyes (Low Tolerance).

My Own Journey

As a child in England, I was fascinated by the correlation between people's face shapes and their behavior. When I shared these observations with my mother, she said, "Don't be so silly, you're imagining things."

In 1981 my interest was rekindled when I took a color course with the late Suzanne Caygill at the Academy of Color in San Francisco. Suzanne was the "grand dame" of the color industry. Her ability was far beyond any color system developed during or since that time. No one came close to matching her talent. It was fascinating to watch her creating individual color charts for people. As each fabric swatch was selected, it was magical to watch that person unfold in the range of colors, textures and prints selected. To my knowledge, no one else in the world has developed such a unique typing system. Today there are just a handful of her students still practicing as color consultants.

On graduating from Suzanne's Academy, I began to work with private clients helping them develop their professional wardrobes. After consulting with a few hundred clients, I noticed a distinct correlation between the colors selected for clients and their personal preferences. For example, red pigments indicated whether an individual preferred contemporary or antique furnishings, rounded, oval or angular furniture. I observed that tapered fingers indicated the person looked better in blue-based reds rather than yellow-based reds. There were very few exceptions. Prints that make people look better reflect the contours within the face. Have you ever held up patterned fabrics next to your face and the prints looked horrendous? And other times, the patterns were very flattering? Have you ever wondered why? Well, the prints we look good in are repeating the designs in our faces.

Along with an interior designer, I was hired to help a couple decorate their 6,000-square-foot home. After looking around the house I did not see anything that represented Alan, the husband, other than a painting of sheep at the top of the stairs. When I mentioned this to him he said it was the only item he had purchased on his own. He felt thankful that someone recognized that he was not represented in the home. His wife's geometric influence was noticeable throughout the home in the furniture and accessories. The place lacked Alan's lightness and playfulness and he found the environment very "heavy" and stifling. Alan told me that under much protest from the architect, he changed the design of the balcony from square to round because it didn't feel right to him. This rounded design could also be seen in the painting of the sheep he chose for the stairway.

Innately, we do know these personal preferences. However our intuitive sense often gets smothered, usually beginning from the time of our birth, through the school years, and as we grow into adults. We are influenced by other people's well intended advice or comments that often may cause us to repress our natural knowingness. This applies to the career choices we make and the hobbies we enjoy. Have you ever shared with someone what you would really like to do, and the response is "that sounds boring," or, "what do you want to do that for?" or, "it'll never work." When those types of responses are constant throughout our lives we begin to doubt ourselves. We start to internalize other people's opinions and beliefs and begin thinking this nonsense is really true! Then we start to experience inner conflict, our "learned behavior" and as our "natural knowing" battle each other.

I first came across the Jones system of reading faces after migrating to the West Coast of the U.S. After working as a color consultant, I began to see even greater application for what I had learned. Like many, when I first learned about face reading I was very skeptical because it sounded like another "California fad." After listening to my friends and hearing their excitement at having their "charts done," curiosity got the better of me. With some hesitancy, I made an appointment with a face reading consultant, making sure no one except my husband knew what I was about to do. I was amazed at the accuracy of the reading. I immediately saw how the information could significantly contribute to the quality of people's lives.

FACE READING IS JUST ANOTHER TOOL THAT WILL HELP US TO BETTER UNDERSTAND OURSELVES AND TO BE MORE CONSCIOUS OF OUR COMMUNICATION AND INTERACTION WITH OTHERS. IT HELPS US TO UNDERSTAND OTHERS SO THAT WE CAN LEARN TO LISTEN RATHER THAN REACT OR MAKE HASTY JUDGEMENT.

To many, reading faces may sound outlandish. But there is real scientific evidence to support the accuracy of these

YOU CAN READ A FACE LIKE A BOOK

observations. One cannot ignore confirmation that is staring us in the face (no pun intended). Besides, we all read faces anyway and make snap judgments based on how people look. The face is full of information. Why pretend it doesn't exist? Are we afraid of what will be seen?

My request of you is to be willing to explore and test out the information written in this book. Keep in mind this is an introduction to reading faces and it only discusses the extremes. When the traits are neither high nor low the person will exhibit both behavioral tendencies. There are many traits not included in this book. These are the traits that are covered in the advanced studies. They require supervised training in order to accurately assess them.

NOT A PSYCHIC

Many times I have shared a few quick observations with people, based on what I see and what I know. Sometimes people think I have some extraordinary psychic ability. This is not so. The information I gather is purely from looking at people's physical features. I only work with the information I have before me and I have found the conclusions to be extremely accurate.

DOES FACE READING APPLY TO OTHER CULTURES?

Yes, the major differences would be the flare of the nostrils, protruding lips and wide-set eyes. According to optometrists, the spacing between the eyes of people with Asian and African heritage tends to be ten percent wider than in the Western world. These differences are taken into account when determining the significance of any feature. You will find many people with Asian backgrounds have wide-set eyes, which indicates they are very tolerant. Now, I did not say patient. To be tolerant is one's ability to put up with situations for a long period of time. Impatience is an irritation in the moment. This tendency is determined by the inward slope of the forehead located at the outer edge of the eyebrows.

Over the past few years there have been several books published on face reading. They appear to be very generalized with little or no research behind them to back up their theories. They come across as light entertainment rather than a reliable source of information or of practical use. This does not refer to books published on facial expressions, only the physical features.

The major difference between these other theories and the Jones system is the extensive research that isolated 68 features and their characteristics. Accuracy rates of 88% or higher are based on feedback from thousands of clients. This includes in-person consultations as well as profiles made from photographs.

To back up these findings, my husband created a computer program for determining careers based on the facial features. The software matches people's physical features to career profiles. These profiles are based on client interviews for career profiling and a book published by the U.S. Department of Labor in 1991 called the Dictionary of Occupational Titles. The book describes abilities needed for specific jobs such as people skills, research, organizational skills and attention to detail. I have found our career matching program to be very accurate for people of all cultural backgrounds. We have named the program the Career and Personality Assessment Profile (CAPA).

Many people come to me because they are experiencing frustration with their current job or are in a mid-life career change. Having tried many other career evaluation tests, they are seeking alternative solutions to finding the right career. I have worked with a number of graduate students who are still looking for the ideal career. After they get the results their response has been, "where were you when I needed you?" It is also possible to do this with photographs. I receive photos from all over the world. The feedback from my clients indicates the profile is at least ninety percent accurate.

Exploring other areas of aptitude or personal interest only enriches life's experiences and adds value to the career finally decided upon.

However, according to psychologists, at least 80 percent of the workforce are in jobs they do not enjoy. Many people in their late forties and fifties have stated they hate their job, but the job pays the mortgage and puts food on the table. These discontented people are counting the days to retirement.

Why are people so off track? Parents have significant influence on the choices children make. Parents want their sons or daughters to follow in their footsteps or to find a career that pays well. Often artistic pursuits are discouraged, just as they were with the boy in the movie, *Billy Elliot*. In the movie, Billy's father frowned on the idea of his son dancing. It wasn't the "manly" thing to do. It took some time and determination before the father realized how talented and passionate his son was about dancing.

A young Chinese college student desperately wanted to be an artist. She took some art classes in college; however, her parents thoroughly disapproved and wanted her to become an engineer instead. She followed their wishes. Despite her efforts to enjoy engineering courses, it was a struggle for her to get through them. Eventually the opportunity arose for her to do some illustrations for one of the classes she was taking. She loved doing the drawings! This was the turning point in her life. She resumed her artistic studies and went on to become a very successful artist and sculptor.

A NOTE TO PARENTS: LISTEN TO YOUR CHILDREN, FIND OUT WHAT IGNITES THEIR PASSION. IT IS THEIR LIFE AND IT'S THEIR DREAM; AS PARENTS WE NEED TO ALLOW OUR CHILDREN THAT FREEDOM.

The innate abilities and characteristics we inherit are only one of the forces controlling our lives. Early nurturing and the experiences of life strongly shape our personalities. Of course, after childhood we can still, by conscious desire and choice, change our attitudes, behavior and activities.

We are born with certain easily recognizable physical features. There are some changes that occur as we grow older, including frowns and mounds that develop above the eyebrows – the result of constantly frowning and tensing the muscles. Perhaps the job they are working on requires high attention to detail or getting things "exactly right." If the individual is not detailed by nature, detailed work will be a constant struggle for them. The shape of the mouth may also change. This often occurs when individuals keep in their feelings pent up over a long period of time.

On its own and without any childhood reinforcement, a behavior may not be that significant, particularly if it is not a strong one. However if this trait occurs in combination with other traits, the effect may be strongly modified or amplified. For example, if a person is extremely aggressive and forceful, these traits may become moderated by traits that foster consideration towards others.

Another example: Individuals with narrow faces are usually hesitant about approaching new situations without prior knowledge or experience. However if they are risk takers, and very competitive, they may find themselves out on the edge and wondering why they do this to themselves.

You'll Never Look at Another Face in the Same Way Again

Face reading is a very simple and uncomplicated exercise. What you see is what you get. The traits discussed in the book are the ones that can be easily determined by simple observation. Does the person have a wide or narrow face? Is the hair fine or coarse? Do they have full or thin lips? Is the nose pointed or rounded?

Professional face-readers use specifically designed tools for measuring face and head proportions. These tools are not needed for non-professional spot analysis, however. It would require a formal training program for anyone to become a qualified expert in the field, and charge fees for consultations. There are training programs and workshops available in the United States and Europe.

There are far more structural/behavioral patterns to discover. This book is just the beginning. I've attempted to give you enough information so you can start learning more about yourself. Discovering what makes you act in certain ways. Understanding why you experience certain emotions. In this way you can live closer to the "examined life" that Socrates spoke of centuries ago.

Throughout this book I will be relating real-life stories and responses from people with whom I have worked. I interviewed more than 500 people and have discovered how challenged people can be when they have some of these traits, particularly when traits are in conflict with one another. Study one trait at a time until you have fully mastered the concept. I should warn you, however, you will never look at faces in the same way again.

KNOW THYSELF

Understanding your own traits is the first step toward becoming the individual you want to be. This book does not claim that the information performs miracles, nor does it claim that you will magically transform into a completely fulfilled human being. What it can do, however, is provide an introductory map to assist you on your personal quest, not for ultimate answers, but toward an understanding of yourself so you may learn how to relate and communicate with others more effectively. Learning how to identify the clues in your face allows you to glimpse at the possibilities and get in touch with who you are, rather than buying into the belief systems that others may have imposed on you.

In a world where many people spend their lives doing things they hate, face reading will give you vital clues as to what you are innately gifted to do. For example, the rounded outer rim of the ear indicates a love of music. Individuals with square chins love debate, are good at mediation, or enjoy fighting for a cause. Small lines that flare out from the inner corner of the eye suggest an innate ability to write.

Take time out and find a quiet space. Think about the things you enjoy. What thoughts stir up? What generates excitement or passion? Is it an activity, a favorite place, the aroma of old books or buildings that brings back the nostalgia of times in the past? What were your dreams as a child?

The purpose of this book is to introduce some of the well-researched personality traits that will help you gain a better understanding of yourself and people throughout the world. Study one trait at a time and notice, when people have a certain trait, how they respond to situations or how they behave. Look for the patterns.

CHAPTER ONE: THE ASYMMETRICAL FACE

THE ASYMMETRICAL FACE

Mood swings

Note the number of differences from one side of the face to the other.
The more asymmetrical the face, the higher the mood swings.

Faces are not symmetrical. How we see ourselves in the mirror versus how other people see us may be quite different. To see the difference between the right and left side of one's face requires close examination.

The more apparent the differences between the two sides of the face, the greater are the mood swings or the inner conflicts that can exist. As I mentioned earlier, this is the result of the parents being significantly different from each other, structurally. The child inherits physical features from each parent. The lower right (base of chin to eyebrow) of the face and upper left (from the eyebrow to the top of the head) reflects the father's traits, and the lower left and upper right side of the face reflect those of the mother's.

They can be all for something one moment and in the next moment they have changed their mind. They are enthusiastic with the start of a new day and then suddenly they feel unsure of themselves, possibly even depressed. These swings are as confusing to the individual as they are to the people they live with. Individuals with these mood changes can be unpredictable and very complex people. Sometimes these mood changes can last for a few hours, sometimes several days. The more a person's life is out of balance, the greater the mood swings. This is frustrating and confusing for everyone – the individual having these experiences as well as the people they work and live with.

A couple of friends decided to go on a sailing trip together. I forewarned one of them that his sailing partner could be emotionally explosive at times, based solely on my observations of his physical features. I advised him not to take the situation personally but find ways to smooth it out. After the trip, my friend expressed how valuable it was to have that information prior to the trip. Since he was forewarned, he was prepared when the outbursts occurred. Had he not known or suspected this behavior, it could have ruined the whole trip. They were able to get through the more challenging moments and had a great time, with plans to go out again.

There are several ways to manage these mood changes. Many of my clients have found exercising or engaging in an activity they enjoy helped to bring them out of the low moods. For me, I like to go on four-mile walks. Some people find yoga significantly helps to balance them.

If you experience mood swings ask yourself, "what can you do now that will help you get back to a more positive frame of mind?" Create a plan – for the next hour, or for the whole day – that will keep you moving toward this more positive place. Don't just "stew in the mood." Take action now. Think about the impact your mood is having on others. How would you feel about being with someone who is having a moody moment? Would you want them as a companion?

When people get caught up in an emotional set of circumstances, a higher degree of sensitivity will result. Things that seemed right before will now appear wrong. What was tolerable before becomes intolerable. People will become more irritated and wonder why they are feeling this way. They perceive something must be wrong with them. When these mood swings occur it's best for that person to just "go with the flow" rather than feeling tense or depressed about the situation or trying to fight it. Take a look at your life, what is missing for you right now. Listen to some relaxing music, go for a walk or a bike ride, or take some time out to visit with friends.

Those of you who do not experience these mood changes may think this is all very strange. Many a person has broken down when he/she learned what could be causing the emotional imbalances in their life. They had been dealing with this situation for years, not knowing quite why they were so changeable. It was never severe enough to seek professional help so they just plowed through life somewhat puzzled by the changes. Once this tendency had been identified they could now do something about the situation.

On the positive side, people who score high on mood swings have a much broader range of interests and are very versatile. They may go through several successful career changes in a lifetime.

THERE IS ALWAYS CHOICE

Although we have inherited our physical features and certain personality traits, we can choose to control our behavior and the way in which those traits affect others around us. Once the traits are identified, we can consciously choose to suppress a basic urge when it is not appropriate.

For example, someone who has a square chin, who tends to be somewhat pugnacious, might be predisposed toward more aggressive behavior but, once becoming aware of these tendencies, he or she can choose to gain control and channel their energy in more productive and supportive ways. People with this personality trait combination can learn to avoid or remove themselves from situations that stimulate negative behavior.

The choice is ultimately each individual's responsibility.

CHAPTER TWO: THE HAIR

COARSE HAIR   FINE HAIR
Less sensitive   Extremely sensitive

Is your hair fine, medium or coarse? Have you ever thought that your hair could suggest an aspect of your personality?

The texture of the hair determines how sensitive an individual is to sound, touch, taste and feelings. This trait can be determined by using a micrometer to measure the thickness of a single strand of hair near the ear. Typically the thickness ranges from 1.25 to 4.0 thousands of an inch. The thickness can also be estimated by feeling the hair, but this method is less accurate. The finer the hair, the greater the person's sensitivity; the coarser the hair, the longer it takes for situations to get under that person's skin.

Many people assume that people with African or Asian heritage have coarser hair. Their hair has a wide range of textures, just like other races.

Individuals with fine hair are overly sensitive. Their feelings are easily hurt and they are very sensitive to loud noises or anything that is rough and coarse. They can wallow in their hurt feelings for days, especially if they also have close-set eyes. All they think about is what that person said or did to them. To others, these sensitive souls seem to be overreacting. One client told me that if her parents would simply look at her when she had done something wrong, she would shrivel up inside. Loud music, noisy machinery, the grating of a knife across a plate or someone talking loudly will really bother more sensitive people. If the noise continues they become very irritated.

A client of mine reported a time when she was being coached. The coach wanted to make a point and he started pounding on the table. His pounding took the fine-haired client by surprise. She was really bothered by it and had to move away from him, feeling very uncomfortable. A coarse-haired person may not have noticed the intrusion and, even if they did, it probably wouldn't have bothered them as much.

On the phone, fine-haired people's voices will sound very soft, particularly if they also have a narrow face. When giving a talk or making an announcement they need to remember to project their voice so they are heard.

Chris was fine-haired and very passionate about her work, but she wondered why her communications were not getting across. As I coached her, I was able to point out some of the tendencies of the more sensitive personalities. Her voice was very soft and her emotions were not being expressed in her face. I suggested that she "speak up," using more expression in her voice and in her face.

All through Ruth's life she had been accused of being overly sensitive and was told by both her English mother and, later in life, her husband, to "toughen up… it's not proper to show your feelings." When I explained the High Sensitive trait to her she felt she was understood for the first time. Over the years she had withdrawn and felt the only way to cope was to keep her feelings inside her. This could be seen by her thin lips, which indicated she had held back her anger and frustration for years. With some coaching she is now able to manage her tendency to be overly sensitive and emotionally repressed. All she needed was the validation that someone understood her natural responses. Her message now gets across more powerfully and her passion really comes across in her communications.

Fine-haired individuals savor quality rather than quantity – from fine pieces of furniture to delicate china. Elegant dining and traveling in comfort is greatly appreciated.

Many couples who are on the opposite poles of this trait – differences in personal sensitivities – have told me that this is one of the greatest challenges in their relationship. The person with fine hair will see their coarse-haired partner as uncaring and not at all sensitive to their feelings or emotions. The coarse-haired individual sees their partner as overreacting and being too needy. Their attitude towards their Sensitive partner is "toughen up" and, "don't be such a wimp."

With relationships, I find that couples are more compatible when they have similar hair texture.

Camping out is not as enjoyable for individuals with fine hair. They'd rather stay in a bed and breakfast or at a four-star hotel. However, if the camping situation has sufficient comforts then it would be more acceptable to the fine-haired person.

People with coarser hair may come across as being less sensitive. It takes a lot more for situations to get under their skin. They have feelings, but they do not come to the surface quite as quickly compared to people with finer hair. It will take a lot more stimulus to elicit a response from these folks.

In general, coarse-haired individuals are also less sensitive to pain. They find Sensitive people very annoying people. Slobodan Milosevic, the former Yugoslav President, is a good example of the Low Sensitive trait. His indifference to other people's suffering was very apparent.

During a networking event, a woman with coarse hair volunteered her assistance in selling products at my booth. She became quite excited with the results she was generating. She kept punching my arm saying in a loud voice, "See how good I am." By the end of the afternoon my arm was sore. I was embarrassed by her brashness and aggressive selling style.

As you may have guessed, I have baby-fine hair. How do I handle sensitivity? When I find myself in a situation where my feelings are hurt or I see myself as being overly sensitive, I remind myself by giving my hair a gentle pull and saying to myself, "it's your hair… get control of yourself." It's a reminder for me not to overreact.

Individuals with coarse hair enjoy things on a grand scale – be it loud music, large amounts of food, boisterous laughter, stronger sensations and lots of intensity. They love the outdoors, camping and the extreme elements of the sun, wind, rain and snow. If they also have olive green eyes this will add to their enjoyment of outdoor activities. Coarse-haired individuals should get out of town occasionally. Otherwise it will create an imbalance in their lives. They love the ruggedness of the outdoors. A client with this trait told me that when work becomes too stressful she finds that camping really helps her forget all her troubles. She's able to get a better nights sleep in the outdoors than when she's home.

One coarse-haired person told me that she would feel really deprived if she were not able to be outdoors. She spends much of her free time in her garden. She would feel very confined if the outdoors were not available to her.

Many politicians have coarse hair, which gives them an added "coat of armor" against the inevitable criticism they receive. Bill Clinton, Tony Blair, Colin Powell, and Pakistan President Musharraf are some examples. Many corporate CEOs and professional athletes will have coarse hair too. They are constantly coming under criticism and often need to deal with extreme crises. While a fine-haired individual could handle these situations and pressures, after a while, it would wear them down eventually.

Individuals whose hair is neither fine nor coarse will exhibit both tendencies in moderation. They are able to adapt more easily to situations and find it easier to give and take. Just being more aware of the tendencies of others helps them know the best way to interact with them.

⟨⟨⟨⟨⟩⟩⟩⟩

HAVE YOU EVER SHAKEN HANDS WITH SOMEONE WHOSE GRIP IS LIKE A VISE? OR HAVE YOU EVER BEEN HUGGED OR PUNCHED IN A FRIENDLY FASHION AND IT REALLY HURT? CHECK OUT THEIR HAIR NEXT TIME. ODDS ARE THAT THEY ARE COARSE-HAIRED AND HAVE THIS SEEMINGLY INSENSITIVE NATURE. THEY ARE VERY EXPRESSIVE IN THEIR REACTIONS, PARTICULARLY WHEN THEY ARE ENTHUSIASTIC.

⟨⟨⟨⟨⟩⟩⟩⟩

People with a wide range of textures in their hair will find themselves going back and forth in their moods. One moment they will thoroughly enjoy the loud music and another time they will find the noise level unbearable. One such woman I met loves both extremes but only when she is able to handle them. Sometimes she found herself walking out of rock concerts because the music was too loud, whereas the previous weekend the sound level didn't bother her. This really confused her boyfriend who had looked forward to attending the event. Her unpredictable mood changes were a sore point in her relationships.

RELATIONSHIPS

In relationships, it is ideal if both people have similar hair texture. If there are wide differences, there could be many more misunderstandings and hurt feelings. Couples are often forgiving of each other's traits during the courting stages. Later in the relationship, the differences may become no longer tolerable. As one person told me, "If I had known about the other person's traits earlier I would never have entered into the relationship." Should one person have coarse hair and the other fine, the finer-haired person may perceive the other as being rough and loud. The coarse-haired person may be more aggressive in their love making, particularly if this trait is combined with High Physical – a tendency to be more physical, frequently without thought – and the risk-taking trait (ring finger longer than index finger). In turn, the coarser-haired individual could think their partner is being overly sensitive and complaining. Once this trait is understood by both parties, each person can make the necessary behavior adjustments.

I recommend that couples who are contemplating living together or getting married have a Relationship Profile prior to the commitment. This is an assessment I make by interviewing them together. It saves lots of hurt feelings, time and money. Why go through the pain of trial and error when a small investment may help to smooth out or avoid those bumpy times?

CHILDREN

Children with fine hair will get their feelings hurt very quickly. Knowing this about your child will help you understand them better. A young girl with fine hair would run off to her room whenever her feelings were hurt. Her mother wondered why she would suddenly disappear, unaware that her daughter was upset. This was the child's way of coping. If your child has coarse hair, teach him or her to be more understanding towards children that are more sensitive. Teach them to modulate their voices, and not to be so rowdy around others with finer hair.

When there are differences between parent and child, the coarse-haired parent needs to be aware of the effect he or she is having on the fine-haired child. For example, a coarse-haired father may see his fine-haired son as behaving like a wimp. He'll want the son to "toughen up" and act like a man. He needs to avoid the negative comments that can really harm the child. One Highly Sensitive little girl was retreating into her shell because her stepfather was being very aggressive towards her. He was unaware of his effect on her. Once he became aware of his stepdaughter's nature, he took a softer approach. It is particularly important to be aware of those differences if the parent is a stepfather or stepmother, or the child is adopted or lives with a foster parent.

SALES

If you are in sales and your client has fine hair you might want to emphasize the quality of the product. If you have a loud voice, then speak in softer tones. In the event the place is noisy, you might suggest you go somewhere that's quiet to have your conversation or make your pitch. Showing them this consideration will really work for you. The coarse-haired person will not be as affected by the noise level. Use a stronger voice and bigger gestures with the coarse-haired individual. Everything needs to be emphasized on a larger scale.

FAMOUS FACES · COARSE HAIR

Bill Clinton, George W. Bush, Chelsea Clinton and Halle Berry.

CHAPTER THREE: THE HANDS

On arriving at the Seattle airport, I went in search of a taxicab. I had hardly stepped out of the airport when a cab came zooming up to me. Hmm, that was quick, I thought. I got into the cab and off we went at high speed. I took one look at the driver's hands and forehead and tightened the seat belt and grabbed something to hold on to. I knew we were about to break all records. My driver also appeared to be very sleepy, although that did not seem to slow him down. I felt a great sense of relief as I stepped into the safety of the hotel driveway. I left him with the parting words to slow down.

RISK-TAKING

RING FINGER LONGER
THAN INDEX FINGER

High risk-taker

INDEX FINGER LONG
THAN RING FINGER

Low risk-taker

The Risk-Taking trait is determined by the length of the ring finger compared with the length of the index finger. This feature is best viewed with the palms of the hands facing toward you or, if you are looking at your own hands, stand in front of a mirror. The fingers need to be touching each other and the knuckles straight. If the ring finger is longer than the index finger, this indicates you will enjoy taking risks. Risk will give you a natural high, a rush of adrenaline. The risk can be financial or physical. If there is a difference between the two hands in the finger measurement, it indicates that at times there is a more cautious side to your nature and other times you will love to take risks. If both ring fingers are shorter than the index fingers, this suggests you are a more cautious risk taker. You will look at all the odds before taking risks.

Risk-taking could be anything from adrenaline-releasing physical activities like skydiving, to more intellectual and passive ventures such as speculating in the stock market or gambling. High-Risk people enjoy the thrill that risk-taking brings them. Sometimes they are willing to risk all, without considering the consequences. Such was the case of one couple, where the husband was an impulsive gambler and lost everything they owned, including the house. The marriage also suffered and a divorce followed.

When risk-taking is combined with a sloped-back forehead, the individual with this this combination will love to drive fast cars. One client I met said his dream was to own a hot rod. When Mark was sixteen, he really loved to race cars around the fields and later won many car-racing competitions. After a serious accident he was laid up for months, yet this didn't stop him from racing. It was an exhilarating experience that required a lot of focus. It gave him a "buzz" unlike anything else. After his car crash, his new job did not give him the same level of satisfaction. His other love was to trade in the commodity market; he stated, "when the time's right you just do it." This year alone he bought 22 flats in London, betting on the market going up. He invested up to the hilt. It's the thrill of risking all that drives him, without it he felt life would be very dull. He does not look at his ventures as real risks because he feels he is able to manage them.

Individuals with high-risk trait enjoy being on the edge of life. They may sell drugs just for the high level of excitement it brings them. One man I interviewed, whom I'll call Jack, said he had an addiction to spending, however, once he made the purchase, whether it was expensive clothes, a car or whatever took his fancy – grief sets in because the excitement has gone. He got a high on making big purchases but it only lasted for a short time, then he felt empty. The thrill of taking such a risk left him flat and life lost its appeal. As a football player, he enjoyed taking physical risks, that was what the game was about for him. Other risks included flirting at a risky level, it is a game for him, and he has very little fear of anything.

⌒≈⋙⋘≈⌐

STEVE, WHO USED TO BE IN THE POLICE FORCE, SAID HE ENJOYED SERVING WARRANTS BECAUSE OF THE POSSIBLE RISK FACTOR. KICKING DOWN DOORS HEIGHTENED THE ELEMENT OF RISK – IT GAVE HIM A HIGH. HE ENJOYED BEING IN THE MIDDLE OF THE FRAY OF THINGS. AS A YOUNG MAN HE LOVED STREET DRAG RACING WITH FAST CARS. FOR SOME PEOPLE THERE MAY BE NEVER EVER ENOUGH RISK; THEY DO SOME PERILOUS THINGS FOR THE NEXT RUSH THAT IT WILL GIVE THEM. THEY FIND IT STIMULATING TO BE LIVING IN THE UNCERTAINTY OF LIFE.

⌒≈⋙⋘≈⌐

Ann stated she loved to invest her money in high-risk investments. Her attitude was, "No skin off my back, just go for it." Her husband also enjoyed taking financial risk. This was a challenge to their financial planner. For them money had no value other than for making for large purchases. Ann shared the time when she and her husband went white-water rafting. She fell out and was caught under the raft by her life vest and her husband, who could not swim, also tipped out of the raft. Even that didn't dampen their enthusiasm. They went right back the next day and continued the rafting trip. Another time she and her husband went hiking in the mountains. As they were coming back down from their trip, she saw fresh mountain lion prints along with their own. Rather than feeling scared she was thrilled by the experience.

Risk-taking for Eva included bungee jumping, which gave her a total feeling of complete surrender. When she jumped off the bridge, she said it was "awesome." Once the element of fear was over, she tried in every way to get a new experience, a new high. She did not know whether she would live through it, but she thought why not anyway? "Just let go." She finds risk-taking is exhilarating; it taps into her aliveness. She loves to coach others to take risk. Risk also includes emotional risk, sharing and telling the truth, baring the feelings.

If you are a Risk Taker, consider how the risk could affect other people's lives. Participate in a sport or other activities that satisfies your need to take chances. Do not expect Low Risk Takers to eagerly embrace your passion for risk. If you enjoy gambling, make sure you keep within your budget, particularly if you have family responsibilities. Many relationships have been affected by out-of-control gambling. Ask yourself, "Is it worth the gamble to lose what I have?"

CHILDREN

A note to parents: if your children enjoy risk-taking activities, make sure they have the training needed prior to their participation. At least you will feel more relaxed and the chances of their being injured will hopefully be reduced.

It is important to recognize the risk-taking trait in teenagers, or they may direct this need in a negative direction such as buying and selling drugs, racing cars, robbery or shoplifting. Channel their energies into sports or other activities that have an element of risk. The reward for risk-takers is the exhilarating experience. This is hard to understand for parents whose traits indicate a more cautious nature. When we recognize and support these needs in our children, it will help us to guide them through the more challenging years.

Individuals at the opposite end of the pole, the Low Risk Takers, take more calculated risks – they have a conservative approach. They will first consider all aspects of a situation before taking a chance. A risk for these people could be changing jobs, living in a new city or participating in a new activity. The activities they perceive as risky may appear dull to those people who are Risk Takers. This is by simply participating in a new activity, they are operating out of their own comfort zone. Risk-taking is on a different level for them. If you are more cautious and there is some element of risk in what you are about to do, familiarize yourself with what it entails. This will help you approach the situation with more confidence. Don't dampen the enthusiasm of people who are seekers of the unknown.

When an individual has a trait combination of Risk-Taking, narrow face and Competitiveness (head wider above the ear), he/she will feel driven out on to the edge of things. This is a scary situation. They experience a strong driving force that pushes them forward. It's like being out on the edge and wondering what on earth are you doing out there.

HAND DEXTERITY

THREE MIDDLE FINGERS
SIMILAR IN LENGTH

High hand dexterity

THREE MIDDLE FINGERS
DIFFERENT IN LENGTH

Low hand dexterity

Dexterity is determined by the three middle fingers. With your palms facing you and the fingers together, take a look at your three middle fingers. Are they similar in length? If so, this indicates High Hand Dexterity.

People with this trait have more innate skill since they can grasp and manipulate objects more effectively. If the ends of the fingers are also square this will add to their skill. This person would be a natural "handyman." We see this trait in car mechanics, carpenters, sculptors, massage therapists, dentists, and artists. If you are not a natural "handyman," then hire someone else who loves to do that work.

This innate ability to work with one's hands will be heightened if he or she also has fine hair, a rounded outer edge of ear (Music Appreciation) and straight eyebrows (Aesthetic Appreciation). These people find the "hands on" experience very meditative.

I asked a dentist who had these traits why he chose dentistry as a career. His response was, "I enjoyed working with my hands and this was a profession where I could generate a reasonable income doing just that."

If your children have High Hand Dexterity, buy them toys that require the high hand dexterity and precision that will help them build on their natural skills. Support and acknowledge them when they achieve results, even though those results may not come up to your expectations. If Johnny has an innate ability to do well in arts and crafts and Sean finds it's a struggle to do half as well, encourage Sean into another activity where he can excel and point out the merit of each to both children.

I have met many people who have followed their parents' advice about a career, only to feel frustrated and unfulfilled later in their lives because their parents' advice was not in line with their own individual traits. Others have rejected all the advice and followed their own hearts, despite the lack of support of their family or friends. They frequently report hearing comments such as, "you'll never make any money from doing that," "How are you going to support yourself on such a meager income?" or "Your father was a lawyer and we want you to follow in his footsteps." Can you relate to this? Do you look forward to going to work each day with enthusiasm? Many don't.

CAREERS

Massage therapist, chiropractor, physical therapist, dentist, hair stylist, carpenter, auto mechanic, and musician.

HOBBIES

Woodworking, sewing, stenciling, quilting, pottery, sculpture, making jewelry, painting, mosaics or playing a musical instrument.

INTENSE FEELINGS AND EMOTIONS

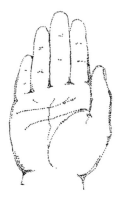

THUMB COMES UP TO FIRST JOINT ON FINGER
Explosive emotions and anger

When the thumb reaches the first knuckle of the index finger the person may have explosive emotions or anger. They feel emotions more intensely. In order to observe this feature, the fingers must be straight and touching each other. The thumb should be resting against the index finger. It is important to make sure the fingers are straight, just glancing at someone's hands when they are slightly bent may give the wrong appearance.

Individuals with this trait can explode in the moment. The anger and emotions come to the surface very quickly and will take people by surprise. It goes as quickly as it comes on. As people mature they learn to hold back their anger. They have realized it can get them into trouble. Individuals with this trait may strike out at whatever infuriates or threatens them. They may want to hurt whoever is causing them a problem. Often the target of this anger is within the family. However, as with all traits, there is choice in how we handle our reactions. This trait is also about having control, so if the situation is getting out of hand and people are not doing what was told or agreed to, this person could explode very quickly.

Sally had prepared a stew for the evening meal. It had been simmering on the stove for a long time. Her well-intended mother-in-law thought it was done and turned it off. This really made Sally see red. She saw this as one more act of interference. In a rage, she took the stew off the stove and poured it out on the garden. This is a good example of the trait out of control. Another possible approach could have been for Sally to take a moment by herself and calm down before actually doing anything.

This personality trait appears to be more male-dominant and the physical feature that indicates it usually appears on the right hand, occasional on the left hand, and sometimes on both. I met a man who had this trait – both thumbs came up to the knuckle on his index fingers – in both hands and his resulting behavior had caused problems in all of his marriages. The positive side of the trait is that these people will come to the rescue when danger is threatening another person. We hear about great feats of individuals lifting cars off people who have been pined down in an accident. This is the kind of energy that erupts from these types of people. One way to channel this energy is to exercise – work out at a gym, cycle, play a sport that requires physical stamina, or lift weights. One gentleman told me that when he exercised he felt more balanced and in control of his energy. When challenging situations confronted him, he was able to handle them better. Or, if he found his anger about to erupt, he would deliberately go for a walk to calm down.

This is an important trait for children to understand and manage. It helps them find a way to defuse their anger before it gets them into trouble. If this trait is combined with Low Tolerance and Backward Balance (more head observed behind the ear as seen from the side profile), this could be an explosive situation waiting to happen, par-ticularly if the person has been raised in an abusive environment.

PHILOSOPHICAL

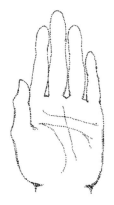

GAPS BETWEEN THE FINGERS

Interested in philosophy

Around 3000 BC, the Egyptians observed that there was a strong correlation between the gaps between the fingers and people's philosophical tendencies. When the palms are viewed with the fingers together against the light, you may be able to see a certain amount of space visible between the fingers. The larger the gaps or the amount of light you can see between the fingers, the more philosophical the person is. These individuals are continually searching for the answers on a spiritual and soul-searching level. The larger the gaps, the greater the search. They are restless until they get a sense of their own balance and fulfillment. They have an innate sense for spiritual values and seek a purpose beyond material levels. These people may go on a lifelong personal quest to seek a lifestyle that gives them a deeper meaning and satisfaction.

Many individuals with the philosophical trait like to surround themselves with stacks of books on philosophy. They will study at length to find their inner journey. In some instances, they may go as far as traveling to India to study under a guru to find their answers. They may even retreat to a monastery. Individuals who possess this feature, in combination with fine hair, close-set eyes, high forehead (intellect), and sharp, pointed features, may become so caught up in their searches that they lose sight of what is happening around them.

Many are fascinated about learning various stories of life; they will often look for their answers in alternative religions such as Eastern philosophy or Native American Indian philosophy where spiritual traditions are linked to the relationship with spirit and earth. One individual said she now uses art to address some of her philosophical questions; she finds answers through her art.

An event called the Groove Garden is held once a month in Fairfax, just north of San Francisco. At this popular event, people can either listen to soft relaxing music in the meditation room or enjoy freeform dancing in the adjacent room. The softly lit rooms are draped with large parachutes which adds to the ambiance of the evening. It's a great place for people to escape from the usual bar scene. There is a noticeable profile in common with the people who attend the event, which is philosophical (gaps between the fingers, fine hair, and narrow faces). Many a time I have said to someone from Marin County, "I expect you go to the Groove Garden." Needless to say they are quite amazed and wonder how I could possibly know. Some common profiles are easier to spot than others.

CAREERS AND HOBBIES

Interests include the pursuit of evangelistic or philosophical issues and metaphysics. Occupations such as the ministry, or leading philosophical workshops and seminars may interest them.

FAMOUS FACES · PHILOSOPHICAL

Muhammad Ali, Julia Roberts and Andre Agassi.

SOLITUDE

SHORT HEART LINE

The Hermit

Some people just need some time by themselves. This trait is the horizontal line on the palm of the hands that is near the base of the fingers. The line usually ends just below the index finger (Notice the short line in the sketch). Once they have recharged, individuals with this high need for solitude can be very sociable people. The other person in the relationship may feel cut out of their partner's life at times and can feel unwanted.

Many people with this trait enjoy activities that give them the time they need to be alone. My husband, Andrew, loves to fly his model airplanes in a remote area with no one around. He enjoys having the space just to himself. Ann likes to work in her herb garden because it gives her the space she needs.

Amanda is familiar with a high need for Solitude. She found her need for people and her need for her own private space to be a dichotomy with which she had to come to terms. This push-pull made it difficult to create balance in her life. One moment she needed people around her; then suddenly she hit the wall and did not want to interact with people, and needed to escape into her own space by herself. When she reaches a point of saturation, she often takes off in the midst of a social event. This puzzles her friends because they want her to stay around for a while. This is a challenge in relationships. When she wants her boyfriends to leave, she wants them to go "right now." This behavior tends to confuse them and they feel rejected. These extremes have left her feeling very confused; at times, Amanda thought she was crazy. She started to see a therapist but still did not find the answers. When I explained the trait to her, she felt the lifting of the weight off her shoulders. It made sense and the internal struggle was less. Will this knowledge change her? Only if she develops an awareness of the push and pull of her traits. At least knowing what's going on will help her to better understand herself.

Another client with this trait told me that if she doesn't have some space to herself she feels claustrophobic and overwhelmed; being by herself gives her a chance to replenish and renew herself. She placed high emphasis on needing time to be alone.

Children who have this trait may disappear off into their rooms or a secret place in the garden, just to be by themselves. As parents, we need to respect their space. If the child spends too much time alone, then there would be cause for concern.

CHAPTER FOUR: THE LEGS

SHORT LEGS (LONG WAIST)
Built to be on their feet

LONG LEGS (SHORT WAIST)
Can sit for long periods of time

Jennifer's desk job often creates an issue in her life. She needs to be up and moving around rather than sitting down at a desk all day. There comes a point in her job when she can't stand it any more, and her mind stops functioning – especially when she has to write up a tedious report. She finds that going for a walk helps to relieve the irritation of sitting for so long. Unless she does this, she finds numerous mistakes in her report. Just stepping outside for a moment helps her to concentrate better. So the next time someone says to you, "I hate my desk job," check out the length of their legs.

LONG V SHORT LEGS

To determine your leg proportion, stand in front of a mirror to see if your legs are longer in proportion to the upper torso of your body. If you are looking at another person, notice if their upper torso is shorter or longer in proportion to the length of their legs. Simpler still, ask someone if they are short-, medium- or long-legged.

Why is leg length important? Leg length has a direct bearing on career selection and sporting activities. A short-legged individual will have a hard time sitting at a desk job all day; they tend to get very restless, particularly if the space from the base of chin to the base of nose is very long. Many short-legged clients have shared with me that in order for them to sit still for so long they must run, work out at a gym or take a long walk before coming to work or during the lunch hour. This helps individuals with this trait to get through their day. Sometimes the love of the job will override the need to move around; they frequently appear to adapt to the situation. However, after a while these individuals will find themselves getting very irritable and may take their irritation out on their family or friends – seldom on a coworker. One short-legged person shared that running gave him the time to himself. This not only benefited himself, but also his family and employer. His mind felt clearer and his production was up at work. A suggestion to teachers: If there are some children having a hard time focusing or sitting still, take a break and do some stretching exercises in the classroom. This will help to relieve some of the restlessness.

The long-legged person is more structurally suited to sit for longer periods of time and even enjoy a desk job. When individuals with this trait also possess the traits Low Adventurousness (inclination towards change and excitement is low) and Low Progressive (low inclination to move ideas forward) they may be seen as couch potatoes; they're quite contented to spend hours sitting in the same place.

A person in sales had been reassigned to a desk job and expressed how much he disliked that position. His restless nature associated with his shorter legs was part of the reason. Another factor was that he needed more contact with people. Sometimes, part of the job requirement is to sit at a desk; if this is the case for you, and you are a short-legged individual, try to get some exercise either before the day starts or during the lunch hour. You won't feel so restless or become irritated so quickly, and you'll be able to concentrate better.

If you are long-legged and part of the job activity requires you to stand all day, make sure you take short rest periods. If possible, find a seat and rest your legs. When on a vacation, plan a mixture of touring and physical activities. If your travel companion has the opposite build to yourself, work something out ahead of time so that the activities are something you can both enjoy.

WHEN YOU ARE GOING OFF ON A LONG-DISTANCE HIKE OR ANY ACTIVITY THAT REQUIRES SOME STAMINA, MAKE SURE THE OTHER PEOPLE INVOLVED HAVE THE SAME ABILITY AND DESIRE. THIS AVOIDS DISAPPOINTMENT.

Individuals with short to medium legs find that walking is a good exercise for reducing stress. If possible, try to select an environment where you feel the most relaxed – such as by the water, out in the open spaces, or in a wooded setting.

CHILDREN

Children generally develop their proportions by time they reach kindergarten. The child with a longer torso can be distinguished at birth. The parents should guide their children into activities designed for this body type. Well, you may ask, what about basketball where most of the players are long legged, almost a requirement for the game? Long-legged children/teenagers need to take more time out during the game to stay fresh and avoid the back problems they may experience later on.

Parents, if your child has short legs and wide-set eyes, encourage him/her to play sports as soon as possible. One short-legged woman I met said that during her early years at school she was constantly in the principal's office for disrupting the class or for bad grades. When she reached junior high school and started playing sports, her grades improved immediately.

RELATIONSHIPS

During a weekend in Yosemite, my husband and I, along with some friends, decided to hike up Half Dome. We had hardly climbed a mile and a half when our friends decided they'd had enough and wanted to go back down. This was somewhat disappointing, so the next day we agreed to go our separate ways and meet later in the evening. Our friends took a bus tour and we hiked up to Half Dome.

When couples do not share these traits, there can be disappointment when certain activities are not mutually enjoyable. Find a way to reach a compromise and understand that each person enjoys doing different things and to reconcile to it.

If we were to conduct a study of professional athletes we probably notice some similar facial features and leg length within the same sport – even within the positions that were played. I met a female professional soccer player who plays goalie for her team. I noticed that when I looked at her face her eyelids were exposed. This indicates that she likes to take action right away. After that observation I started to look at other goalies. Many had that trait. Other features suggest this trait – such as Competitive Drive, Risk Taking, Restlessness (long space from base of chin to base of nose) and other physical attributes. This is a trait cluster often seen in professional sports players.

HOBBIES AND CAREERS

Short-legged people enjoy jogging, gymnastics, hiking, tennis, soccer, football, gardening, aerobics, wrestling, or mountain climbing.

Careers might include sales, construction, waiting tables, beautician, nursing, hockey, coaching sports, serving in the military or any job that requires standing.

Long-legged people enjoy cycling, swimming, golf, dancing, volleyball, yoga, high jump, pole vaulting, ice skating or ice dancing.

FAMOUS FACES · LONG LEGS

Tennis players Venus and Serena Williams, Nicole Kidman and Shania Twain.

FAMOUS FACES · SHORT LEGS

William Macy, Pierce Brosnan, Hugh Grant and Monica Seles.

CHAPTER FIVE:
THE EYES — WINDOWS OF THE SOUL

EMOTIONAL EXPRESSION

LARGE IRISES

High emotional
expression

SMALL IRISES

Low emotional
expression

For most of us, the eyes are the first features we look at when we meet someone. They send many messages. Are they open and welcoming or "beady" and suspicious? Do they dart about? Is the person telling the truth? People with sparkling eyes are more approachable. They look friendlier. Individuals with cold, piercing eyes appear to be looking right through us. The eyes send signals we unconsciously read and make judgements from based on past experiences. Children have large irresistible irises with a wonderful look of innocence. We all want to reach out and touch just to be close to the affection that pours from their eyes.

One woman I met had cold piercing eyes; she felt very misunderstood by people and wondered why. It took a while for people she met to move beyond what appeared to them to be a coldness; yet underneath was a very warm and caring person. If you find yourself reacting or turning away from certain people, give them a chance. Get to know them first. Then decide.

EMOTIONAL EXPRESSION

The amount of emotion that a person will express is determined by the size of the iris in relationship to the sclera (white of the eye). The larger the iris, the more likely an individual will be to show and express what they feel. People with large irises tend to be very emotional and are generally more open to sharing their feelings and emotions. They are very affectionate. They display their feelings, whether showing sorrow, happiness or enthusiasm. At times they are overly emotional, especially when this trait is combined with Low Tolerance and Dramatic tendencies. These individuals will "fall in love" within the first few minutes, maybe even seconds. They can get so caught up in other people's emotional situations that they can become emotionally drained and exhausted. When emotions are running very high the situation can be completely blown out of context. This will be exaggerated with the Low Tolerance trait (close-set eyes).

John stated that his wife needed high emotional maintenance. She needed to be reassured several times a day that he loved her. Her emotional needs were very high, not because she was insecure, but because she was a very emotional person. If her husband did not express his affection toward her, she would think she must have done something wrong, or, worse, he didn't love her any more. Or heaven forbid, maybe he was having an affair!

When Susan felt very pleased with the project she had completed at work, she related it to the times when "she had to show mom that she had cleaned her room." In this case, she sought out her supervisor to show him what she had accomplished. She needed his approval. If acknowledgement was not forthcoming, she felt really let down. As a child, she often felt her emotions were not reciprocated. Living in the city drove her crazy; she saw so many homeless people, the stress was too much for her. There was so much to be done, and she couldn't save the world. She was so overwhelmed by the situation that she found herself staying inside rather than being reminded of the suffering going on in the city.

If you tend to get overly emotional about other people's problems or situations, step back and try not to get so involved.

CHILDREN ARE GENERALLY BORN WITH REALLY LARGE IRISES; HOWEVER, WHEN THEY ARE LIVING IN WAR ZONE AREAS SUCH AS AFGHANISTAN, ISRAEL, BOSNIA AND OTHER AREAS OF EXTREME UNREST, YOU WILL NOTICE THE WHITES OF THE EYES ARE EXPOSED UNDER THE IRISES. THIS INDICATES THE CHILD OR ADULT IS UNDER A LOT OF STRESS. IF THE WHITE SHOWS UNDER ONLY ONE IRIS, THIS IS THE FIRST STAGE OF STRESS. IF UNDER BOTH, THIS IS LONG-TERM STRESS ALMOST TO THE POINT OF THE PERSON BECOMING VERY MELANCHOLY.

People with small irises do not let their emotions sway them in their decision-making. They are able to deal more dispassionately with others. They make decisions with their head rather than the heart. Their eyes are less expressive and they run the risk of appearing indifferent, cold or unemotional. They keep their feelings hidden under the surface. Low Emotionally Expressive people are not as outwardly affectionate and find it difficult to express what they feel. They stay outwardly calm and work well in situations where emotions are getting out of control. They pride themselves on their emotional control. Often times this trait will indicate verbal, physical or sexual abuse in their past.

Encourage the less emotional individuals to express themselves more. It may be difficult at first for them, so suggest they take one small step at a time. They may feel psychologically naked, revealing all for the world to see. It might be hard for them to break down the protective barrier they have built around themselves and their feelings.

It takes a while to get to know these individuals. Over the years they have learned that people just don't seem to care about their feelings so, rather than risk rejection, they keep their emotions to themselves. In personal relationships this can be somewhat challenging. Everyone else could be breaking down emotionally around them and they will pride themselves on not showing how they feel. They may see others as appearing weak.

One High Emotional Expressive man who also had the magnetic eyes (the amount of warmth and sparkle in the eyes), shared with me that he was very good at fund raising. He was very persuasive and was able to solicit large sums of money from people. He reassured me that he never took it too far but admitted at times it was very tempting. He knew the power of his persuasive charm and did not abuse it.

FAMOUS FACES · HIGH EMOTIONAL EXPRESSION
Raquel Welch, Jennifer Aniston, actor Tim Henman.

MAGNETISM

EYE SPARKLES	NO EYE SPARKLES
High magnetism	Low magnetism

The deeper and the more sparkling the eye color, the more magnetic the personality. This is not to be confused with the Emotional Expressive trait that is related to the size of the iris. Magnetism has to do with the eye color and how much sparkle is in the eyes. Just as with High Emotional Expressive, when we meet people who have sparkling eyes, we are immediately attracted to them. Strangers will pour out their life stories to these individuals. Men and women who have these magnetic eyes are thought to be flirtatious and inviting sexual advancements. One woman I interviewed said she found it annoying when men came up and flirted with her; she thought they had some ulterior motive. In her early twenties, she tried to look as unattractive as possible in order to turn people off.

Many a couple has told me that this flirtatious quality was a huge issue in their marriage. Tom was convinced his wife Carole was deliberately flirting with other men at parties or any social gathering they went to. It was at the point where Carole no longer wanted to go to any parties because it became such a conflict between them. She often felt strange because men would constantly approach her, believing she was flirting with them, while women avoided her because they felt threatened by her seemingly flirtatious behavior.

If you have magnetic eyes, use body language to avoid unwanted attention. Make it clear as soon as someone advances toward you that you are not available. Take a couple of steps back, physically distancing yourself from the person. Fold your arms or use a firm voice. If your partner gets jealous, ask them how they would feel if you exhibited the same level of jealousy towards them. Find a solution that you can both work with before the situation gets out of hand.

In sales situations, these magnetic eyes stir up the emotions, especially if the sales person also has low-set eyebrows. These features – along with the competitive trait– are great assets in sales. If your client has magnetic eyes, notice the amount of expression in their eyes. This will tell you how the sale or presentation is progressing.

I met a woman at a workshop who had very cold-looking eyes, extremely high-set eyebrows and exposed eyelids. She was surprised that I came up to her because people did not usually approach her. She often felt misunderstood and isolated in social gatherings. If you have this trait combination or know of someone who does, suggest they wear flattering colors or seek out a color or image consultant. The proper colors really helps to soften such an austere message and will help individuals who appear very formal, to look more approachable. Low magnetism often reflects a negative environment. These individuals may have been exposed to conflict or abuse within a family, war zone or anywhere that stress is a part of a person's daily life.

CHILDREN

When children have High Magnetism, they quickly learn how to take advantage of this asset by appealing to the parent who is most susceptible. Parents, as adorable as your children are, make sure you stay within the boundaries you have set for them. Children will constantly test those boundaries to see how much they can get away with.

CAREERS

High Magnetism is a great trait for salespeople. They can be very persuasive, especially in face-to-face negotiations. This is also an advantage in counseling and the ministry, and romantic roles in the theatre, and for workshop leaders. It is a great asset to have when you are working with people.

FAMOUS FACES · MAGNETISM

Jimmy Carter, Mel Gibson, Richard Gere and Julia Roberts.

A note from my editor: evidence published in scientific journals finds a significant correlation between people's eye color and behavior. These differences were first noted in the animal world. In the 1970s, psychologists were able to correlate it to human behavior. A simplistic overview: people with light-colored eyes are better at self-paced activities; people with dark-colored eyes are better at reactive activities. For instance, in basketball, players with light-colored eyes tend to have better free-throw shooting records because it involves standing in a stationary position and shooting when the individual is ready; dark-eyed individuals tend to be better at rebounding, a reactive activity. In baseball, light-eyed individuals tend to have better pitching records, because pitchers throw the ball at their own pace; dark-eyed players tend to be better at the reactive skill of fielding balls.

TOLERANCE

NARROW SPACE
BETWEEN THE EYES

Low tolerance

WIDE SPACE
BETWEEN THE EYES

High tolerance

Tolerance is one of the most important personality traits. It indicates the timing of the emotional response and reaction in the moment. Tolerance has nothing to do with impatience. Rather, it indicates how long an individual will put up with a situation before they respond. How much he or she will let things deviate from the way they should be done before doing something about it. This trait is determined by the spacing of the eyes. Individuals with close-set eyes will react to situations more quickly and will want to work by the rules. Wide-set-eyed individuals are extremely tolerant and laid back.

In order to accurately determine this trait, we first measure the space between the eyes, then we measure the width of each eye. This is to determine which is the larger of the two. If the eye is bigger or the same size as the space between the eyes, this indicates the person tends to be Low Tolerant. If the width of the eye is smaller, an individual will be a lot more tolerant.

High Tolerant individuals (wide-set eyes), are more permissive, both of themselves and of others. They appear to be very easy going and have a tendency to put things off until tomorrow. They often put up with situations for too long and need to set more boundaries. People tend to take advantage of their good nature. They come across as being very relaxed. Individuals with this trait almost

YOU CAN READ A FACE LIKE A BOOK

welcome interruptions. If their friends or client's arrive late for an appointment this does not tend to bother them. Because of their laid back attitude, these individuals tend to be very popular. They are easier to work with. This trait is often seen in political and business leaders, and in careers where the individual needs to handle or oversee a number of ongoing projects.

When working with High Tolerant people, make it known that they need to complete the project on time. Let them know why the project is important and the consequences of delaying its completion. Create benchmarks. This will help them to stay focused. When individuals with this trait are late, try not to snap or glare at them. Find out what you can do together to speed up the process.

Individuals with this trait tend to get easily distracted and take on too many projects at once. They over extend themselves and consequently find themselves running late for appointments because they want to do "just one more thing" before they leave their homes or offices. Their friends and associates may see them as unreliable when, in fact, they are really trying to fit in too many things at the last moment. Their challenge is to stay focused on what they are doing and not get caught up with unrelated projects or activities.

If you have the High Tolerance trait, make sure you arrive on time for appointments. If you find yourself running late, call ahead of time to let the other person know. This trait also indicates that you like to work with the big picture. Make sure you set boundaries and deadlines, and stick to them. Think first before committing yourself to yet another project.

Mary said she finds it very difficult to concentrate and becomes very scattered. She starts on one thing and then suddenly switches to something else. While making the bed she suddenly gets distracted by the pet dog and takes it for a walk, then goes on to something else without finishing the previous project. Or when she is working on a business-related project, there's a tendency for her to start off on one project and before she knows what's happened, she moves on to the next or gets completely sidetracked. If you fall into this category, create a list of the things you need to do and stay with each task until it is completed.

Have you ever noticed that when you're just leaving on a trip with family or friends, that there's often someone who has just one more phone call to make? Or they tend to take forever to get out of the door? Needless to say, this is really annoying to Low Tolerant individuals. The person waiting in the car for them starts honking the horn trying to create a sense of urgency. This is not a good way to start out on a trip.

Low Tolerant people are more focused on the issue at hand. They have an intense "now" reaction and a built-in sense of right and wrong. When they are focused, nothing else exists for them. If you need their attention, give them some time to break away from what they are doing. This

INDIVIDUALS WITH CLOSE-SET EYES ARE GREAT WITH DETAILS. I ONCE RECEIVED A CALL FROM A "HEADHUNTER" WHO WANTED TO KNOW WHAT TRAITS TO LOOK FOR WHICH WOULD INDICATE IF A POTENTIAL CANDIDATE WOULD BE GOOD AT DETAIL. IN THE PAST HE HAD HIRED PEOPLE WHO STATED THEY WERE GOOD AT DETAIL, BUT ONCE ON THE JOB THIS WAS NOT THE CASE. AFTER GIVING HIM THE PROFILE TO LOOK FOR, THE PROBLEM WAS SOLVED.

will help to avoid irritation or being snapped at. If these individuals are presented with too many tasks at once, they get very frustrated and overwhelmed by the pressure. One client stated that when he gets into overload, he shuts down and closes his door to be alone. Otherwise he finds himself snapping at people and then gets hard on himself. That is not how he wants to be towards others.

Another client shared that when she gets really hard on herself when her tolerance goes. She does not feel her behavior is appropriate. She is equally intolerant of other people's behavior – people breaking rules that she doesn't allow herself to break. Whereas, an individual with wide set eyes would be more likely to say, "Don't worry about it this time. Who's to know?"

If you are a low tolerance person, you may be over reacting without realizing it. Things annoy you more quickly, so relax and take a deep breath, find a way to release your intense feelings. Re-focus your thoughts, look at the situation from a different perspective. Remember your perspective may be different than that of others.

Melanie was facing a challenging situation with a coworker that was causing her a lot of stress at work and in her personal life. She attended one of my teleclasses. During the call, we covered the Low Tolerance trait, which she was able to relate to. After the call, she realized how her Low Tolerance trait was affecting her communication at work. The next day, rather than insisting things had to be done her way, she was more open to considering a different approach. It worked. She felt a huge load lift off her shoulders.

Sally said she is thrown off at work when a plan has been made and suddenly it is changed. She likes to stick with what was agreed on. What would work for her would be if the other person making the change said, "What do you think about this?" Then she could be more flexible and counter her automatic no. Or, "Here's another way to look at it," would also make her more receptive. When Sally's routine was interrupted by a chattering coworker, she would feel very annoyed and would become quickly rattled. If they just said, "Can I talk to you for a minute" that would be better than just butting in to her routine. She found tolerance was her biggest challenge. Her father was very rigid and one of her fears was having a child that would have the same personality as her father.

The Low Tolerant person is quick to respond, fast to react and very intense in his/her emotional involvement or responses. This intensity is often seen in people who follow a cult leader or have very strong religious or spiritual beliefs. Close and deep-set eyes can be seen in many followers of the Taliban and religious cult members. Low Tolerant people become so focused on their beliefs that they fail to notice what else is going on around them; they lose perspective. When there are a number of people in the same group or meeting with this trait, there may be tendency to fuel each other's passions, taking them deeper into their intensity.

At times, the Low Tolerant individual will seem overly fussy about the smallest details. This will be exaggerated if they have a pointed nose and tight skin over the frame of the forehead. Individuals with this trait combination will appear to be overly obsessive about neatness. Several women I interviewed with these traits expressed their frustration when their husbands left "their stuff lying around." Whenever they tried to throw out things that were "garbage" from their point of view, their husbands would retrieve these items from the trash. They resorted to putting the objects in empty cereal boxes to disguise them and even asked their neighbors if they could use their trash can! These women were obsessive about clutter. When I asked what they would do if their husbands threw their stuff out the response was, "I'd kill him." Then I asked them, "How do you think he feels?" There was a long pause of surprise.

Typically, people with fine hair (very sensitive) and close-set eyes (Low Tolerance) become so focused on what is wrong or upsetting them, they will tend to get things out of context. Their thoughts immediately go to, what is wrong and they'll worry it over and over in their minds. If this is something you can relate to you might want to find an activity that will take you away from your concerns, such as practicing yoga or listening to your favorite music.

Individuals with Low Tolerance make good teachers, lawyers, dentists and supervisors. They are intolerant of error. They instantly perceive what is wrong and get quickly irritated by interruptions, sloppy workmanship or tasks not being done on time. They have a sense of right or wrong, and have the advantage of always being aware of what should be permitted. We may find that this trait is observed in some of the people who commit road rage. They will have less tolerance for what they perceive as "stupid drivers."

Let's not forget the positive side of the trait. These people make excellent teachers because they stay focused; they're not as scattered. They are great with detail. Wouldn't you want your dentist, editor or accountant to have this trait? So if you're not good at detail look for someone with close-set eyes. If they are also critical, this will heighten their awareness of mistakes. When I first met my new dentist I was very relieved to see his eyes were close-set.

This trait is often seen in tennis players and golfers, where focus on the ball is extremely important throughout the game. We certainly saw John McEnroe's Low Tolerance on the courts when he was an active player.

CHILDREN · HIGH TOLERANCE

The wide-set-eyed child is very easy going and quickly gets distracted from what they are doing. This can be challenging at school. They forget to do their homework, feed the dog or to tidy their room. If you send them on an errand that should only take a few minutes, they come back an hour later. Parents need to set deadlines for the child and make sure they are kept. Children with this trait need to be given boundaries; homework must be done first before they go off and play with their friends. No phone calls or visitors until chores are done.

CHILDREN · LOW TOLERANCE

If your child tends to be Low Tolerant, provide time for him/her to break away from what they are doing; the transition will meet with less resistance. Just taking this approach will help to avoid much of the conflict experienced when children are interrupted without warning. One little girl had traveled some distance with her parents for her appointment with me. When I explained to her parents about the "Five-minute warning," the child responded by saying, "Just my parents knowing that, was worth the trip." It had definitely been a challenging issue between parents and child.

When school children have a combination of High Tolerance and High Physical Motivation (long lower face) they will have a very short attention span. Until the child and parents understand that this is a part of the child's genetic make up, this trait cluster may be interpreted as disruptive. Mandy had this trait combination. She found it very difficult to concentrate in her early years at school. She was constantly in the principal's office and failing in her schoolwork. At age 13 she went to junior high school and started playing sports. This was a turning point in her life. From that moment there were no more problems and she immediately excelled in school. Sports had not been a part of her life prior to that time. If the parents had known earlier, they could have enrolled her in an after-school sports program.

This could also be an explanation for some of the attention deficit (ADD) problems. We may find that for some of these children, sports or other activities will help to channel the energy, making a significant difference to the quality of their lives.

SWING ON TOLERANCE
When the corner of one eye is closer to the center of the nose than the other, this indicates a swing tendency from Low to High Tolerance, and vice versa. Individuals with this mood swing will be mostly on the tolerant side. However, when things get too much for them they will suddenly "snap" – out of the blue. They

feel guilty at losing their cool and then are hard on themselves for being so intolerant. If you have this trait and you find yourself in this kind of situation, take some time out, focus on what needs to be done, and don't get caught up in the overwhelming situation. Typically when there is a swing in this trait, it seems to often come from the paternal side of the family.

RELATIONSHIPS

Tolerance is so important in how two people get along together. When there is similar tolerance in relationships, the couple will have similar points of view on what is right or wrong. If they are on the opposite poles, the Low Tolerant person will be irritated by the laid back, easygoing, High Tolerant attitude of his or her partner. What was forgivable prior to moving in together now becomes irritating. The High Tolerant person will see the opposite; the partner overreacting and perhaps cramping his or her more laid-back style of living. If you are the High Tolerant partner and find yourself running late, call ahead of time and let the other person know. If your partner asks you to do something, only agree to do it if you really intend to. Otherwise the Low Tolerant person will nag at you for not following through.

FAMOUS FACES · HIGH TOLERANCE

Richard Branson, William Hague, Brad Pitt, Boris Yeltsin and Hillary Clinton.

FAMOUS FACES · LOW TOLERANCE

John McEnroe, Cher, Monica Seles and Barbra Streisand.

UNCONVENTIONAL

INNER CORNER OF THE LEFT EYE HIGHER THAN THE RIGHT EYE
Unconventional

When the inner corners of both eyes are on the same level this will indicate the person is fairly conventional. If the inner corner of one eye is set higher than the other this indicates unconventional judgment. Less conventional individuals do not like to do things the way others do them; they find it very boring. Their challenge is to compromise when working with more conventional people. The greater the differences between the two eyes, the more the person with this trait will want to travel the unconventional path.

When Ron meets a woman he immediately makes a judgement of details like the hair is too short or the earrings don't work. This has really bothered him all his life because he felt it wasn't good to be constantly judging everything. He found living with his Unconventional trait to be very challenging; he was always judging people and, at times, it got in the way of him making friends. He even went as far as researching this tendency to find out why he was this way. Nothing he found could explain it. The fact that I was able to recognize it right away gave him some comfort that it wasn't something he had made up. As he suspected, it was a part of his genetic make-up.

We all judge people and situations to some degree. However, Unconventional individuals will have a judgement about everything. This will include the quality of something or how something should or should not have been done. People who are more conventional tend to be less judgmental and are more comfortable with a conventional approach.

Individuals who are less conventional are very creative and come up with new ideas or solutions to problems. We would expect to see this trait in the film industry, writing, art or any situation where this creativity can be used. They enjoy a less conventional approach in personal relationships. They need to be aware that not everyone will be comfortable with their approach. They need to be willing to compromise.

CHILDREN

Children with this trait may make a name in history later on if their unconventionality can be directed constructively. The parents' job is to help them to direct the trait in a positive direction so it becomes second nature for the child later in life.

RELATIONSHIPS

Less Conventional individuals with this trait will enjoy novel approaches in their lovemaking. If this trait is also combined with high sex drive, and their partner is not meeting their needs, they may well seek affairs outside of their relationship. If you are being tempted to do this, think of ways to re-direct your drive. Take up a hobby that will consume your energy, such as sculpture, painting, woodworking, film, photography or any activity that will satisfy your unconventional approach to life. Or get involved with a sports or fitness program.

CAREERS OR HOBBIES

The Unconventional person is gifted in creative and artistic fields such as invention, art, film, graphics, designing, writing or any profession that could benefit from this ability.

ANALYTICAL

EYELID COVERED WITH FOLD OF SKIN	EYELID COMPLETELY EXPOSED
Loves to analyze	Likes to get to the point

How analytical a person tends to be is determined by how much or how little the eyelids are visible. If the eyelid is completely covered by the fold of skin this will indicate the individual is extremely analytical (High Analytical) and will want to know how and why everything works. Be prepared for lots of questions and be able to back up your statements with facts. On the other hand, individuals whose eyelids are completely exposed (Low Analytical) will want to get directly to the point once they have understood the concept. This can be determined by their direct questions and the desire to get to the bottom of an issue. When you hear this in their voice and conversation, recognize they are ready to make the appointment, purchase the product or do whatever is necessary to get things accomplished. Low Analytical people get very impatient with long-winded discussions or meetings. They like to get the meeting over and done with. If they run the meeting you would expect it to be completed in half the time.

HIGH ANALYTICAL

This trait is determined by the epicanthic fold – the fold of skin that covers the eyelid. High Analytical people need to look into all aspects of a situation or new purchase before making a decision.

They will over-analyze what they already know, and to others this may seem a waste of time. They like to put other "spins" on what is being said. Low Analytical individuals will get very impatient by this painstaking analytical procedure; their response will be, "Come on, let's just get on with it." Whereas Analytical individuals love to take things apart and figure out how they work. They will not only study how the building or equipment was constructed; they'll also want to go into every aspect of the project in order to understand why it was designed that way. When making a new purchase, they will research and compare quality, performance and price. Combine this trait with close-set eyes and sharp features, and you will know this person will want to investigate everything until they are completely satisfied they have all the possible information.

People who are more technical or are researchers will have this High Analytical trait. When buying a car or a piece of equipment, they will want to know down to the smallest detail about how and why it functions. Be prepared for lots of questions. If they also have a pointed nose, they will dig into everything until they are satisfied. Salespeople would do well to have a printout of all the possible questions and answers for prospective individuals with this trait to read. If you are presenting a new product or idea to the customer and you notice they have this trait, you might want to begin your presentation by stating, "You look like a person who will have lots of questions." Present them with a product sheet; they will feel comfortable having the facts literally in hand, and will be less likely to interrupt your presentation.

The High Analytical person will enjoy games such as chess, bridge and crossword puzzles. If the individual with this trait also has sharp features, they tend to be extremely picky. This combination of traits plus an oval forehead are often seen in people in the health-related professions, such as nutritionists, dietitians and chiropractors. Individuals who are analytical and have pointed features make good investigators or FBI agents. This trait combination is a plus for any profession where investigation is part of the job profile. They will turn over every stone until they are sure they have left nothing to dig up.

Sometimes having the High Analytical trait will overcomplicate things. There is tendency to overanalyze simple situations and make things more complicated than they are. For example, something was wrong with my iron. Now, you might think the first thing to check would be the plug. However, for my husband, who is a very analytical, this solution was too simple. He took the iron completely apart and carefully labeled each piece. He could not uncover the problem. I said, "Did you check the plug?" I opened up the plug and there lay the answer – the wires had separated!

If you are very analytical, spend less time analyzing when it is not necessary. Speed up the process. Understand that not everyone needs to know all the details in order to make a decision. Get to the point quickly. If you are on the phone and the person appears to be cutting you off, this could be a signal that the other person on the other end of the line wants to get to the point. This is an important trait to listen for if you if you are in sales.

I received a phone call from a man whom I thought was making general inquiries. After a few minutes he said "Naomi, I just want to make an appointment." Hmm, I thought, this man must have exposed eyelids. Sure enough, when I met him I saw that my assessment had been accurate. I might have lost the sale had I continued talking to him and embarked on a lengthy explanation.

If you are meeting with someone and you have a number of questions, cover the most important ones first. Then, if there is enough time and the person wants to pursue it further, go over the remaining issues.

RELATIONSHIPS

Imagine being with someone so analytical that they have to know the reason for every little thing you do! If you are a Low Analytical person, after a while you'll begin to get fed up with everything being thoroughly questioned. You may just be sharing some news item that you read that day in the local paper, but the analytical person will immediately want to know the facts, where the information came from and was it from a credible source. All that out of sharing some local news. To those of you who are High Analyticals, this may seem reasonable. However those with the opposite trait become quickly annoyed.

LOW ANALYTICAL

People who are Low Analytical do not need to know all the reasons for something up front, just enough information to make a decision now. They like to go directly to the heart of the matter. They will go back later and check the details if needed. Once they have grasped the concept, they prefer to act right away without asking too many questions. They will ask "why," but will not necessarily take the time to deeply analyze the problem. Long drawn-out explanations are boring to them. They are more matter-of-fact and to the point.

Individuals with this trait will appear to be unflappable as they forge ahead in their careers. They may appear to be ruthless and cold because they like to get to the core of things quickly, ignoring the subtleties and different facets which others have meticulously researched for them. They like to cut through the red tape and get things accomplished. Once they understand the general idea, they will want to take action and move directly to the point. In order to do this, they will sometimes cut people off in the middle of a conversation. Others may find these actions rather rude, and considered that what they had to say was of little importance to the Low Analytical person.

There is a tendency with Low Analyticals to interrupt or even finish sentences for the other person. They can also come across as very aggressive – having what has been described as an "in-your-face attitude." Often, such a person is trying to get others to see their point has the opposite of its intended effect since people can be put off by their posturing.

Jennifer's husband constantly interrupted her. She found this really annoying. She would ask him, "Why do you keep interrupting me? I haven't finished yet. Why don't you want to hear what I have to say?" Her husband's response was, "I already know what you're going to say. If only you would just get to the point!"

Nurses and doctors who have the Low Analytical trait love the fast pace and the amount of action in the emergency wards at hospitals. They like the excitement of what is going on around them and enjoy the feeling of rising to the occasion. They like to cut through the red tape in order to get things done. In these situations they are highly productive in their actions.

When Low Analytical Sandra runs a meeting she immediately determines: what's the issue, what's the problem and what do we need to do? This should only take 20 minutes, bam, bam, bam, as far as she's concerned. If others in the meeting want more discussion, her response is, "Why do we need to keep talking? Let's get to work" Sandra doesn't need all of the story before starting on the project. She quickly gets a sense of what needs to be done. A lot is accomplished at her meetings, although some people probably feel more thought and discussion are needed on certain issues.

David was often away from home attending meetings. He called his wife daily to see how her day was going. She would respond with lengthy descriptions of her day. David often cut her off because he didn't want all the details. She felt she was not being heard or that he was not really interested in what she had to say. She was deeply hurt. As a means to avoid her feeling cut off or unappreciated, he would begin his daily calls by explaining that he was between meetings and only had two minutes. It worked; she gave a very brief summary of her day and no feelings were hurt.

If you are more a bottom-line person, understand that others may need to know more information before making a decision. Slow down your reaction time. Be prepared to explain in more detail to people who are more analytical. In a selling situation this will create a feeling of trust. When you ask individuals who are more analytical to take on a task, they may bombard you with questions. They have a compulsion to know more about your request. Try not to cut them off in mid-sentence, make it known up front that time is running out.

FAMOUS FACES · HIGH ANALYTICAL

Tom Hanks, William Shakespeare, James Coburn and Margaret Thatcher.

FAMOUS FACES · LOW ANALYTICAL

Hillary Clinton, Madeleine Albright, Whitney Houston, Michael Caine and Anthony Hopkins.

CRITICAL PERCEPTION

OUTER CORNER OF EYE
LOWER THAN INNER CORNER

High critical perception

OUTER CORNER OF EYE
HIGHER THAN INNER CORNER

Low critical perception

There is a critic in all of us. However, this behavior will be extreme when the outer corner of the eye is lower than the inner corner. People with High Critical Perception tend to see every little error and wonder why others do not see obvious mistakes. Nothing annoys them more than when other people are careless and overlook the obvious. These people are your perfectionists. They not only expect perfection of themselves but also of family members and coworkers. Within the family, the High Critical trait can have quite an impact on the children – who can never seem to please their High Critical parents. Nothing is ever good enough. If the outer corners of the eyes slant upwards, the individual will notice what has been achieved rather than what is wrong. They are far less critical.

Michael's father, who had inherited the Critical trait, never gave his son any positive recognition, no matter how hard Michael tried. Michael could never live up to his father's expectations. He was constantly being criticized. The father felt his son would never amount to much, and told him so. When Michael later spoke to his father about his constant criticism, interruptions and never allowing him to finish what he was saying, the response was, "Your grandfather was a bastard, so I'm a bastard." He felt that justified his attitude towards his son. Later, Michael decided to enroll in a coaching course. This helped him immensely in coping with his father's negative attitude. The next time Michael met with his father he refused to enter into the usual line of fire; consequently, his visit was much better. Even though his father still went through the same dialogue, Michael was able to step back and not engage in such a way that he was fueling the fire.

Kate, who had inherited the critical trait, told me that as a child she found her parents to be extremely daunting. She would often find herself tiptoeing around the house to avoid their criticism, which had often made her cry. At times, she found it difficult to hold her head up, and she did not want her parents to see that side of her. Kate thought that if she could be a perfect student – and get straight "A's" – then her parents would really love her. This created a lot of stress for her at school, to the point where she would drop a class if she received a less-than-perfect grade.

When Kate notices other people's mistakes she feels somewhat superior. She can't stand amateur music. The musician's lack of skill ruins it for her. This feeling of intellectual superiority about her, tends to keep people at bay.

Bob – a High Critical perfectionist – was the owner of a construction company. He really came down on his employees when they failed to notice mistakes in their work. He would rant, "You must be stupid not to notice such obvious mistakes. What's wrong with you? Surely the mistake is obvious?"

This didn't exactly boost the morale of his workers. However, once he understood his gift of seeing errors that others didn't see, he backed off, and only criticized the workmanship only when it was vital to the construction. This man also expressed that his three failed marriages were probably due to his constant criticism of his wives' efforts. They could never get things perfect enough for him and it ground down the relationship.

Ken, age 40, heard about my work and sent me his photo to be analyzed. The first thing that struck me about his facial features was the High Critical trait. His physical features indicated that he had two extremely critical parents. Apparently they had practically destroyed his spirit. After looking at his photograph and noting the rounded outer edge of ear (natural musical ability) I e-mailed back and suggested he study music. As a child, his parents had believed that there was no future for him in that field. Despite their opinions, he eventually went to Los Angeles School of Music, only to receive more criticism. This proved to be too much criticism for him and he dropped out of the music program.

Now, as an adult, he has revived his interest in music and is now playing with a local musical group.

If you have inherited the High Critical Perspective, find ways to look for the good first and remember, you can be your own worst critic. Those words, "Never good enough," that flash through your mind, how does that support your personal growth or that of your family members or coworkers? Praise them for what they have done, look for the good first, then make some helpful and supportive suggestions rather than delineating what's wrong. Think about what it's like when someone criticizes you. If you're a parent, praise your child and acknowledge what they have done. If there is something not quite right you might say, "You've done a great job; there's a couple of things that you might want to change. May I make a suggestion?"

If you tend to be critical, use criticism for on-the-job situations. Learn to use it in a constructive way. Remember to give equal amounts of praise and acknowledge when the job is well done. To criticize fellow workers too much will be counterproductive and result in hard feelings. If you are a parent who has this trait, try not to critique your child's work. Praise him/her for what they have done. If you notice something wrong that could affect a project, gently ask if there is there anything that needs to be to changed.

If you tend to overlook mistakes, be more alert for possible flaws on the job. Get a second opinion from those who tend to notice the mistakes. Double check to make sure that you have not overlooked an important fact.

CHILDREN

If you are High Critical and have children, be aware of the impact your criticism is having on your child, as well as on people you work with and your significant other. How would it change your relationship if you were to master this trait? If your children have inherited the critical trait, teach them how to use it constructively; emphasize the gift, not the challenge. As one person put it, she turns off the trait when it's not needed. This is often easier said than done. Teachers with this trait need to be more sensitive when criticizing their students' work; the criticism can be devastating to them.

SANDRA THOUGHT HER HIGHLY CRITICAL MOTHER DID NOT LOVE OR WANT HER BECAUSE HER MOTHER CRITICIZED HER SO MUCH ALL THROUGH HER CHILDHOOD. IT WASN'T UNTIL SHE WAS 30 YEARS OF AGE THAT SANDRA CONFRONTED HER MOTHER, AND ONLY THEN FOUND OUT HER MOTHER HAD TRULY LOVED HER ALL THAT TIME. HER REGRET WAS THAT IT TOOK HER 30 YEARS OF HER LIFE TO KNOW THAT HER MOTHER TRULY CARED.

CAREERS

In a positive light, this trait is a gift. Individuals who have critical perception would make great editors, cameramen, surgeons or any profession where precision is needed. Wouldn't you want these people as your airplane or car mechanic? Wouldn't you want your surgeon to have this trait? High Critical people make good literary critics, film and music critics, and art critics, particularly where an analytical capability can add insight and perspective.

If you are Low Critical, be more aware of flaws on the job. Get a second opinion from those who tend to notice the errors. Double check to make sure that you have not overlooked an important fact.

FAMOUS FACES · HIGH CRITICAL PERCEPTION

Hugh Grant, Mikhail Gorbachev, John Ashcroft and author J.K. Rowling.

SERIOUS

DEEP-SET EYES
Serious minded

Individuals who have deep-set eyes take life, work and responsibilities extremely seriously. At times they feel it is their responsibility to carry the world on their shoulders. They become quickly annoyed when other people appear to be more flippant about situations. If they don't take things on themselves, who will? They feel it is their destiny.

Individuals with the High Serious trait are more thoughtful and reflective, particularly if they also have close-set eyes (Low Tolerance) and fine hair (Sensitive). Small issues become more significant and completely absorb them. They do not always see the humorous side of life and need to lighten up and have fun. If you are a High Serious individual, take up a hobby or physical activity to help yourself relax and have fun.

Individuals who are on the opposite pole of this trait will take situations less seriously and will be more light-hearted.

Joanne, who is very serious, has a tendency to take on everybody's problems. She wants to feel needed and gets really down if this is not expressed. Being that serious leaves her feeling drained and heavy. I encouraged her to imagine stepping into an area where everything feels lighter and to describe that feeling. After a moment she responded that it felt good; "It feels like another person inside of me that wants to get out; it's like being a kid again." If you are a High Serious individual, remind yourself not to take life so seriously and find ways to look at the lighter side of life.

Don't take things so seriously; share the responsibility of the problems you are surrounded by with others.

RELATIONSHIPS

In relationships the less serious individual may feel weighed down by the seriousness of the other person. They may find the level of seriousness too heavy to the point where it may stifle the relationship.

FAMOUS FACES · HIGH SERIOUS

Abraham Lincoln, Mahatma Gandhi, James Blake, Tom Cruise and Cher.

CHAPTER SIX: THE EYEBROWS

The eyebrows – and the areas around them – have much to tell us about a person. The high or low placement of the eyebrows will indicate if an individual is more selective and formal or whether they come across as being more friendly and casual.

The shape of the eyebrow indicates if an individual has a natural feel for the overall design of something. It could be a building, photography or planning a new project. They have a natural feel for what looks good.

DESIGN APPRECIATION

INVERTED "V" ON TOP OF THE EYEBROW
An appreciation for how things are designed

The Design Appreciation trait indicates an innate appreciation for how things are structured, the design of a building, overall plans for a new business venture, interior design or artistic creations. This trait is determined by the pyramid shape which is formed between the middle and outer edge of the eyebrow. An individual with this innate ability has a sense of the overall structure of whatever interests him or her. These are the architects, designers, photographers and entrepreneurs. Individuals with the with this trait enjoy such activities as designing and organizing a project, conducting a meeting or planning an event. They have a feel for how one element adds to another and how each part connects to build the whole impression. They are very conceptual and have a natural feel for the design before the project has even started.

Individuals with the Design Appreciation trait would enjoy such activities as building an organization, developing the groundwork for planning a housing development or creating a pleasing landscape. They have a sense of where the project is going and how to design the overall picture for it to succeed. If this trait is also combined with mechanical appreciation, imagination and esthetic appreciation, this will add to their ability to plan and organize events, projects or anything that involves design and organization.

When this trait is combined with Sequential Thinking, the individual will enjoy taking something that already exists and improving the design or the material. They're not usually interested in creating the basic design.

Children

Parents, if your children have this trait, buy them toys that evoke their creative ability. Sign them up for a class that will teach them how to improve their skills. Find out what interests them.

Careers

Careers or hobbies such as photography, designing and flying model airplanes, and stained glass art are ideal, when the individual has high hand dexterity. Web design, landscape architect or business developer are also great careers.

Famous Faces · Design Appreciation

George Clooney, Will Smith, Colin Powell and James Coburn.

MECHANICAL APPRECIATION

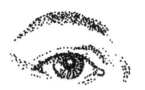

THE HALF-MOON SHAPED EYEBROW

Mechanical Appreciation

Design Appreciation deals with how something is designed. Mechanical Appreciation has to do with the bringing the parts together to make the whole. When the eyebrows resemble the shape of a half-moon, the individual has a natural gift to bring things together. This includes assembling equipment, coordinating a project, organizing an event or bringing a group of people together. Their thinking is very organized. When the Mechanical Appreciation trait is combined with design appreciation, this individual would also make a good facilities planner, interior designer or, with an oval forehead, a project manager. They have a great sense of how to coordinate projects or events and have a real knack with "getting the gears to mesh."

When an individual has both Design and Mechanical Appreciation, they will enjoy working where he or she can translate their innate feel of the situation into a finished project.

Disorganization can get these individuals down. So, if you enjoy having an organized system for your work and surroundings, either hire someone to organize your office for you, or develop a system that keeps your things in order.

CAREERS

Suggested careers are photography, mechanical engineering, sound and lighting technician, fashion design, flower arranging, architecture, organizing closets, carpentry or web design.

CHILDREN

When this trait is seen in young children, their parents should buy them toys that will engage their natural talent for design. Buy them toys such as Lego, puzzles, Tinker Toys or any activity where they can design and assemble objects. Later on it could be computer graphics, stained glass art, or quilting. Encourage them to take up photography or art.

FAMOUS FACES · MECHANICAL APPRECIATION

George Clooney, John Hannah, Wayne Brady and Katie Couric.

AESTHETIC APPRECIATION

UNDERSIDE OF EYEBROW STRAIGHT
An appreciation for balance and harmony

The straight horizontal flat underside of the eyebrow indicates the presence of heightened aesthetic appreciation. This trait indicates the degree to which a person will be moved by the impression he receives through his feelings. These Highly Aesthetic individuals have a great sense of balance and harmony and enjoy being surrounded by beautiful things. It is not necessarily a indication that one possesses artistic ability, however. One can have great appreciation for things without having an innate ability to produce them.

This trait is seen in a number of the more popular male movie stars and male models. Many men and women are drawn to individuals with this trait.

High Aesthetic individuals have intense feelings and appreciation of their surroundings and they tend to do things that will make the environment better for everyone. They rarely raise their voices or make "emotional waves." If unpleasantness occurs, they do their best to manage it equitably for all concerned, unless there is a clash of values.

These people love nature and feel at one with the elements. They have a real sense of the harmony of things, whether it is nature itself, a painting, the way a building is designed or a piece of music. Many of the famous artists and musicians have high aesthetic appreciation.

When the aesthetic individuals' lives are out of balance, they may get caught up in a vicious cycle of turning to what makes them feel good – trying to satisfy their need for balance and harmony in order to dull the discord in their lives. They want to escape from what is irritating and may run away from problems instead of facing and solving them. These are very intense individuals; they will pour themselves into anything they are passionate about to the point where it can become obsessive.

If you're a High Aesthetic individual, your challenge is to identify and deal with the situations that are causing imbalance in your life. You need to be responsible for building your own harmony and can't expect anyone else to do it for you. Don't try to escape it through anger, alcohol, drugs or anything else that can give only temporary release. Be careful not to let pleasing things and pleasurable sensations be distractions. Learn how to create, and leave the world with something worthwhile and lasting.

Sign up for a yoga class; include meditation as a part of your daily activity. If this is not possible, develop a plan to get your life back on track. Hire a personal coach to support and encourage you through your challenges.

CAREERS

Artist, designer, naturalist, collector and environmentalist.

FAMOUS FACES · HIGH AESTHETIC

George Clooney, Mick Jagger and Andre Agassi.

AFFABLE / DISCRIMINATING

LOW-SET EYEBROWS	HIGH-SET EYEBROWS
Affable	High discriminating

The Discriminating and Affable traits reflect the timing of the response to situations that are going on in the moment. If the eyebrow is high set, that person is usually more selective and deliberate in both in their actions and their thinking responses, whereas the person with low set eyebrows will tend to move in on things and act right away.

This trait is determined by the height of the eyebrow in comparison with the vertical height of the eye aperture. When the distance between the top of the eye to the bottom of the eyebrow is greater than the vertical height of the eyelid, it indicates the person will be more Discriminating and come across as being more formal. On the other hand, a person with low-set eyebrows is generally more casual (Affable).

In the Western world, affable tends to be a male-dominant trait, whereas the high-set eyebrow (Discriminating) is more dominant in women. Most people who have Asian heritage have high-set eyebrows. In the studies conducted by Jones, he found that people with high-set eyebrows, regardless of culture, tended to be more formal. Once you get to know them, however, they are very friendly. When you meet these people, shake hands and go through all of the formalities. Then let them make the first move when they are comfortable and ready to become more friendly.

Individuals with high-set eyebrows are more selective about the friends they choose, and the purchases and decisions they make. Don't try to rush them. When shopping for clothes, it may take them a long time before they make a final purchase. These are not impulse buyers. They would rather leave without buying anything rather than purchase something that's not totally satisfactory. They like to make sure it is the right decision before making the final purchase. When they make friends, it is for a lifetime.

When meeting people with high-set eyebrows, step up, shake hands, then step back and allow four to five feet between you unless they initiate closer contact. This also applies to conducting a meeting around a table. Take on a more formal body language, do not place your elbow on the table or lean toward them, unless you really know them well enough to do so. Make an effort to put them at ease and show you are really interested in them as individuals.

Discriminating people appear to be more reserved and less friendly. This tends to build psychological barriers because others may perceive them as being aloof or less approachable. This is not their intention. Many people with this trait have expressed that they feel very lonely, and wonder why people do not readily approach them. I noticed a woman with this trait at a workshop that I attended. She spent much of the day on her own. Noticing this, I went over and spoke to her. She was somewhat surprised because she usually has to make the first move in striking up a conversation with someone. She always felt she was very approachable and could not understand why people did not come up to her.

I have noticed that people in the United States tend to abbreviate names of people they meet without checking to see how that person wants to be called. For instance a person introduces himself as "Anthony" and his name is immediately abbreviated to "Tony." Check with the person first before you shorten his name. He or she may be a Discriminating person and could take offense at this "informalization" of their name. If you are in sales, don't lose a potential client by shortening their name.

Two female professors with backgrounds in international affairs were asked what action other countries would take regarding the peace plan that was being negotiated in Israel. The person with the high-set eyebrows stated, "I think they will wait to see how the situation develops." The person with the low-set eyebrows stated, "Oh, I believe other countries will quickly follow their path." The first professor wanted to survey the situation first, which reflected her Discriminating trait. Whereas the other woman, who was more Affable, thought other countries would move in right away, which reflected her, "Let's move in now," attitude.

Individuals with low-set eyebrows make friends very easily and quickly and show interest in what is happening. They like to make physical contact, such as a light touch on the shoulder, arm, sometimes the knee or even a hug. If they move in too close and too fast they will risk taking the more Discriminating people by surprise. If you are an Affable individual, know when this approach is appropriate. The challenge is to honor another person's space.

APPEARING TOO FORMAL IS OFTEN PERCEIVED AS BEING LESS APPROACHABLE. IF YOU HAVE THIS MORE DISCRIMINATING TRAIT, MAKE AN EFFORT TO BREAK DOWN THE UNSEEN BARRIER. WEAR SOFTER COLORS OR PRINTS; THIS WILL HELP TO SOFTEN THE FORMALITY AND YOU WILL BE SEEN AS MORE APPROACHABLE.

Individuals with low set eyebrows have a more casual approach and often come across as your old friend and buddy. They move in and out very quickly. This can be very confusing to the person they have just met. Business cards or phone numbers are exchanged with the promise to call. To the Affable person this was just a casual contact with no promise to pursue the relationship. The person they have just met might feel confused because they were sure they had just made a new friend and then nothing happens. Often I hear, "I thought this was a new friend….I really liked her." Then there's the feeling of being let down or disappointed. If you have this trait, make it known that this is a casual meeting with no other expectations.

FAMOUS FACES · AFFABLE

Brad Pitt, Pete Sampras, Tom Brokaw, Australian tennis player Lleyton Hewitt, actor Ian Somerhalder.

FAMOUS FACES · DISCRIMINATING

Diane Sawyer, Cher and Hillary Clinton.

CHAPTER SEVEN: THE NOSE

Noses come in all shapes and sizes – some small and cute, others large and very distinguished, although some owners of large noses may not see it that way. Some are pointed; others are more bulbous like Bill Clinton, William Hague and Whoopi Goldberg. In some cultures, noses of a particular shape such as the Roman (convex nose), will be more dominant. This shape is seen in all cultures, although more frequently in the Arab nations. Cosmetic surgery does not change an individual's personality. Michael Jackson has made so many changes to his face it is unclear who he really is; it sends a confused message. If a Roman-nosed individual has the bridge of their nose straightened, he or she will still want to be the boss and will always on be on the lookout for a bargain.

THE MINISTRATIVE NOSE

SKI JUMP NOSE
Enjoys helping others

The ski jump (Ministrative) nose indicates that this individual naturally enjoys helping others and will enjoy working in professions such as nursing, sales assistant, waiting tables and volunteer work. Individuals with this trait automatically respond to other people's needs and requests. They are usually the first people to put up their hands when requests go out for volunteers. They enjoy helping the sick; there is an instinctive feeling for "nursing," especially when combined with High Conservation (oval forehead). If someone needs help, they'll immediately drop what they are doing and will be "right there" for them. Human values come first for them. They put others' needs before their own and sometimes their family's; they need to learn to say no and let others volunteer.

Ministrative individuals have a hard time charging for their services. Usually they are not good at money management, both its use and its value. If they are in business for themselves, they will find the greatest challenge is asking their clients for money. Ministrative individuals are more than likely to say, "Have it for free or pay me next time." The subject of money is the one they like to avoid most; balancing the checkbook is certainly not high on their list of priorities.

If they are in business for themselves, Ministrative individuals might want to have a partner who is good at handling money. I have met a number of people who decided to go into business for themselves and really struggled to make their businesses work – not because they didn't have a good idea or their product was not appealing. They simply did not handle money well. Charging what everyone else is charging is uncomfortable for these individuals.

"WHAT CAN I DO TO HELP?" IS ANNE'S USUAL MANTRA. IT IS HARD FOR HER TO ACCEPT THAT FOLKS CAN DO QUITE WELL WITHOUT HER. SHE IS VERY GOOD AT FACILITATING AN EVENT, AND ENJOYS IT, BUT HAVING PEOPLE REPORT TO HER IS SOMETHING SHE IS NOT COMFORTABLE WITH. DELEGATING TASKS TO OTHERS IS A CHALLENGE FOR HER.

YOU CAN READ A FACE LIKE A BOOK

This was a huge issue for one couple. The husband was such a spontaneous spender that in the end his wife had to set up a separate bank account where he could not touch the money. She decided to give him an allowance or they would have had nothing left in the bank. Ten years later they still have this arrangement.

If these people also have Low Acquisitiveness (ears flat against the head) and a Generous nature (large lower lip), they may give away their last penny. They feel there should be no financial reward for what they do. The focus is on the human value.

Ardelesa, who owns an accounting business, had a really hard time collecting on the money owed to her for her services. In several cases, her accounts receivable had been outstanding for over a year. She knew her clients were short of cash and did not want to press them for payment.

Another person I interviewed said she felt very guilty about charging people; she thought if she was too expensive, her clients would not come back.

Ministrative individuals volunteer their services for nearly every cause that comes along, then find themselves overextended and wonder why. There are times when helping another person simply means that such a person never gets anything done for herself. The challenge is to delegate tasks to others. A vice president of a steel company who had this trait said that managing people was one of his biggest challenges required of his job. It didn't come naturally to him and he had learned how to do it the hard way. It was a position he was still not comfortable with, yet he had no option other than leaving the company. Other people take advantage of this behavior; the Ministrative person becomes their "go-fer." While I was at the company, he was constantly waiting hand and foot on the other departmental vice presidents. He was the first person to help me load up my car.

While visiting Boston, my husband and I got lost. It wasn't long before a woman came up to offer her assistance. She took at least 20 minutes of her time to tell us what sights to visit, how to get there, plus other information about the city. As you may have guessed, she definitely had the ski jump nose. One doesn't need to have a ski jump nose to help others, but helping is a more spontaneous gesture that comes more naturally to these individuals.

If you have the Ministrative trait, keep in mind you don't have to volunteer or contribute to every cause. Learn to "stop doing" for everyone who is needy. Make sure you charge the full market price for your services; don't give your time away or under price yourself. If you charge the full price, people will place more value on what you have to offer. Set priorities and delegate tasks to other people; you don't have to take it all on yourself. If balancing your checkbook is a problem, either hire a bookkeeper or sign up for a class on money management. This would be particularly valuable if you have the trait combination of Low Acquisitiveness (ears flat against your head) and a Generous (full lower lip) individual.

CHILDREN

Children are usually born with a ski-jump shaped nose. If their parents have more convex noses, the chances are the child's nose will be that shape by time they are fully developed.

CAREERS

Nursing, ministry, YMCA, secretary, administrative assistant, volunteer, waiting tables or customer service, social services, hostess in restaurant, and working with children.

FAMOUS FACES · MINISTRATIVE

Singer Geri Halliwell, actor Leonardo DiCaprio, Elton John, and actress Martine McCutcheon.

THE ADMINISTRATIVE NOSE

CONVEX NOSE

Likes to be in charge

The Roman-nosed person wants to be the boss. When this trait is really pronounced, the Administrative individual will also put a price tag on everything. How much does it cost? Is it worth it? Where can I get it for less? Finding a bargain will make their day. They are more concerned with material values and tries to think of ways they can manipulate this to their advantage. To some people they will appear as being impersonal and materialistic. Others may doubt their human or spiritual values.

These individuals are good in finance and business and work best where there is organizing to do, where value for money comes first. They do well at delegating tasks to others and enjoy overseeing projects. Careers such as accounting or appraising and administrative positions would be good for these individuals. They can serve but they would find it very confining to have a career in just a service position. These are not your waiters or receptionists. If you hire individuals with this trait for a predomi-nantly service position they may not last for long or they may end up running the show.

A group of women were complaining about the new hire. The complaint was, "She's already trying to run the department." This was causing bad feelings among the employees who had been there for a while. It was not a good fit. The new employee had been hired for the wrong position.

I was browsing through the market at Covent Garden in England, and nearly all of the store owners had this shape nose. In many of the small convenience stores in London, you will notice most of the shop owners have this trait. During an event in San Francisco, I happened to peek in at a pawn brokers conference. I noticed the majority of the attendees had this convex nose. Next time you pass a pawn brokers you might want to pop in and check the owner's nose! We have a saying that a person has a "nose for money." Now you know what to look for.

It doesn't mean that a person with a concave nose would not be successful in business; neither does it guarantee success if you have a convex-shaped nose. Ministrative individuals will need to make sure they charge the going rate and meet their own financial goals. It can be done; it just takes more determination to make sure the business is financially successful.

If Administrative individual's also has very thin upper and lower lips, he or she will come across as being very tight with money. They won't spend a penny more than necessary, and doesn't like to buy for the sake of it. To others, they appear to be very stingy. One man with this trait combination thought presents were unnecessary; he did not like giving gifts for the sake of it. However, he was quite prepared to spend a lot of money on his favorite hobby.

Janice said her husband had these traits and she found him to be extremely stingy. She thought the stinginess came from family upbringing. While on a trip together, her husband bought two T-shirts, one for himself and one for his wife. Afterwards he asked her to pay him back for her T-shirt. This took her by surprise, as she thought it was a gift. Yes, he was serious about her paying it back.

This trait combination was observed in one of my students. Later, when we discussed this, he confessed he found it very difficult to give. It was too frivolous in his mind. At the end of the workshop, he gave each of us a box of chocolates and said, "I really am trying to be more generous." His gift was greatly appreciated by all.

If you fall into this category, try not to put a price tag on everything, especially within the family. Consider doing some volunteer work and enjoy the reward of helping others who are in need. If you tend to be tight with your money, surprise your partner or friend with a bunch of flowers or bottle of wine or whatever is appropriate. Think of other ways you could contribute. Refrain from putting money and business first. Watch your tendency to be very suspicious, especially with family and friends.

When this trait is combined with a wide face and high-set eyebrows, such people may be seen as being intimidating. You will seldom see this person in the nursing profession unless he or she is the head nurse.

ADMINISTRATIVE / MINISTRATIVE

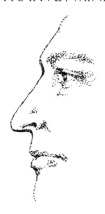

STRAIGHT BRIDGE

Administrative / Ministrative

An individual who has a nose with a straight bridge, has the combination of both the Administrative and Ministrative traits. This trait is often seen in stockbrokers, bankers, middle management and teachers. When combined with the Pioneering trait (straight outer edge of ear) these individuals enjoy business consulting or owning their own business. They have a blend of both serving and being able to administrate over projects but not to the same degree of someone who scores high on either trait.

RELATIONSHIPS

If there are opposites of this trait in a relationship, it may well cause a problem. One will want to spend all the money now while they can still enjoy it and the other person will want to invest it. One will balance the checkbook, while the other person won't know how much is in the account.

CAREERS

Project management (with an oval forehead), investments, accounting (with close-set eyes), fund raising or business administration (this includes any career that involves management and investments), lawyers, business developers, also CEOs and CFOs of companies.

FAMOUS FACES · ADMINISTRATIVE

Abraham Lincoln, John Grisham, Bill Gates, author J.K. Rowling, and Barbra Streisand.

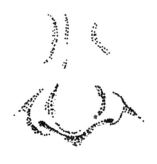

BULBOUS NOSE

Inquisitive

When we think about characters such as Santa Claus (who we called Father Christmas in England), Gnomes, and Mickey Mouse, they all have very rounded noses. Have you ever seen any of these characters with a sharp pointed nose? The sharp nose indicates a very different kind of character. Ebenezer Scrooge is depicted as having a pointed, turned-down nose with very thin lips. In face-reading terms, we would see a person with this profile as being very tight with his money. If he also has cupped-out ears, he will hang on to his money, no matter what. These are probably the people who live with the bare necessities of life and then die as multi-millionaires.

It has been noted that the more round or bulbous the nose, the nosier the person; these individuals are very inquisitive and love to find out the latest information. Other people see this person as being extremely nosy, and who can't keep his/her nose out of other people's business. You may notice when you are reading something and your friend with this curious nose is around, they will often peek over your shoulder to see what you're reading. To some this is very annoying; however, they are merely curious.

Next time someone leans over your shoulder to see what you are doing, before you react first check out their nose. Then quietly say to yourself, oh it's the nose – they are just being curious.

FAMOUS FACES · INQUISITIVE

Jimmy Carter, Bill Clinton, Martine McCutcheon, Colin Powell.

THE INVESTIGATOR

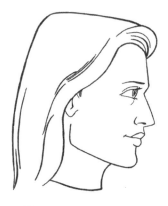

POINTED FEATURES

Loves to investigate

When the nose is extremely pointed, a physical trait revealing an investigative nature, the individual will love to ferret out information. She would do well in careers such as the FBI, fire investigation or any career that would benefit from this natural ability. Such people enjoy investigating and digging below the surface, leaving no stone unturned until they have the answers they are looking for. If these Investigative individuals also have close-set eyes, they will notice every little detail – to the point of being overly fussy. They zoom in on what is not working. They get very upset when a job has not been done properly. If you are looking for a private investigator, this could be the ideal profile. Investigative individuals "follow their noses," and will zero in on the details.

In combination with the tight skin feature, Obsessive, these individuals react immediately to what is going on around them. Their homes and offices would look clinically clean. What would appear to be clean to most people would have them apologizing for their messy home. These individuals will go to the extreme of laying out their clothes for the next day. This trait cluster is often seen in careers such as dental hygienist, nutrition or any health-related field.

FAMOUS FACES · INVESTIGATIVE
    Dick Cheney.

·

THE TRUSTING NOSE

UPTURNED NOSE

Very trusting

The Trusting Nose is determined by looking at the nose from the side profile. When the nose angles up from the underside where it joins the lip (please see sketch), this will indicate a more open-minded and gullible individual. They are often taken advantage of by others and often find themselves falling for other people's practical jokes or schemes. Many people with this trait have fallen under the spell of get-rich-quick schemes. Seldom do you see individuals with the skeptical trait, turned-down nose, fall for the so-called business opportunities that are now in abundance on the Internet.

Individuals with an upturned nose have an almost childlike naiveté. They have a very trusting nature and sorely want to trust others. Even when they have fallen victim to some bad investment scheme, they still want to believe in the good of people. They are easily taken in by others and do not ask for proof before committing their hard-earned savings or time. On the positive side, they are very open minded and receptive, willing to give something "a try." This trait is seen in babies; however, if her parents have the

Administrative trait (convex nose), the child's nose shape will change during her later teenage years.

If you are a more trusting individual, ask more questions until you are completely satisfied before making a final commitment. Do not be taken in by a "good deal." Ask someone who has knowledge about the product or opportunity. Many a person is more trusting and Impulsive have found themselves making a purchase or investment they regret later. They need to keep a little doubt in their minds.

FAMOUS FACES · TRUSTING

Elton John, Jennifer Aniston and Dolly Parton.

THE SKEPTIC

DOWN-TURNED NOSE
Questions everything

STRAIGHT NOSE
Not as skeptical

When the nose turns downward, like those of Meryl Streep, Madeleine Albright and Steven Spielberg, it indicates a Skeptical individual who tends to question everything. Such people do not accept things at face value. They need the proof first. To others, they may appear to be distrustful or even hostile. If you are presenting them with a new concept or idea, make sure you completely satisfy their questions and present them with all the facts first. Once you have done so, you can quickly win them over. Skeptical individuals are often amazed at how trusting some people are; they think it is only natural to question things thoroughly before making a commitment.

Skeptical individuals have a tendency to pour cold water on ideas, a behavior that can crush the enthusiasm of others. That is not their intent; however, it is frequently how they come across to more trusting persons.

This trait can be very challenging in relationships. Skeptical individuals need to learn how to first listen and support someone who shares their ideas with them. Then offer some creative suggestions and caution before taking action or a stand on the situation.

Others may perceive skepticism as criticism and this can bring out defensive behavior. If you are more skeptical, make sure your comments do not come across as being non-supportive to your partner's new idea. Get the whole story and all the facts before judging or making up your mind. Try listening to what the other person has to say first, and then ask them if they would like a second opinion. This will avoid misunderstanding or an emotional response of, "Oh, you never think my ideas are any good."

When you are dealing with Skeptical people, remember, they have the need for proof or substantiation. When presenting them with a new ideas or concepts, make sure you give all the important facts. To them, it appears foolish to accept the ideas at face value.

CAREERS
Judges, lawyers, financial planners, and sports coaches.

FAMOUS FACES · SKEPTICAL
Bob Hope, Madeleine Albright, Ross Perot, many Afghan war lords, and John Lennon.

VERY FUSSY

TIGHT SKIN ACROSS FRAME OF FACE
Likes things to be very clean and neat

When the skin is stretched tightly across the forehead and frame of the face, these individuals are extremely fussy. This picky behavior is heightened if the person also has close-set eyes, is very serious and has a pointed nose. Jennifer acknowledged that she was very picky – the towels had to be folded just right, books had to be angled just right and she can't stand clutter. Yesterday's newspapers on the floor drove her crazy. Anything that was not being used has to be tossed out. When she puts clothing out for the Salvation Army to pick up she makes sure the clothes are folded absolutely perfectly. This is a gracious touch and shows respect for the Salvation Army and the next user.

When individuals are obsessive, they need to be aware of their behavior and be open to doing something about it. Negative comments or pointing a finger at the other person just aggravates the situation.

If you have this trait keep in mind that not everyone has the same need to be so "squeaky clean."

CAREERS

Dietitian, medical science researcher, and pharmacist.

FAMOUS FACES · FUSSY

Dick Cheney, actor Ross Kemp, Diane Sawyer and Meryl Streep.

SELF-RELIANCE

FLARED NOSTRILS

Extremely independent

Self-Reliance is an environmental trait that is determined by the flare of the nostrils. The larger the flare of the nostrils, the more self-reliant or independent the person. The trait is subject to change, according to the conditions that surround the individual in their home and work environment. It also reflects one's own inner chatter – positive or negative. The more determined an individual is, the larger the nostrils flare. High Self-Reliance people often insist on making the decisions, not only for themselves, but also members of the family or people they work with. They are used to doing things on their own and acting independently, and often feel that their way is the right way.

Often times they will take the job away from another person because feel they can do it better and faster. They don't always trust others to do it right, and they get impatient when having to wait around for something that they could have done in half the time.

Individuals who are Low Self-Reliant (pinched nostrils) have learned to hang back and see what others want to do. They give people more space and time to do whatever needs to be done. They work well on teams.

The High Self-Reliant trait can be a problem when working with a team because people with this trait may not accept the authority of other people. They have no idea how others are reacting to their "doing it on their own." Individuals with this trait need to stop and see what is going on around them, and be more sensitive to the people they are working with. They should stop and think about alternative ways of handling a situation.

Low Self-Reliant individuals follow authority well but may relinquish their own authority too soon. They hesitate to do things by themselves, such as start their own businesses. This was the case for a woman who had all of the qualifications and ability to set up her own business. But as soon as she met any obstacles, she backed off. Despite several attempts to start a business without the support from others, she found it very difficult to move her ideas forward. Low Self-Reliant people are not comfortable working on their own. You will not find many with this trait who have their own business and have made a success of it unless they have overcome this tendency. Their inner chatter of, "I can't do it by myself, or "What if it doesn't work out?" will hold them back. If you find yourself repeating these thoughts, try using your mental "delete button" and replace it with positive thinking and action.

If the nostrils are extremely flared, these individuals can be very unforgiving; once you have crossed them. They will hold that against you for a lifetime. This trait was observed in a young man who was in his early twenties. He acknowledged it was a problem and inquired how he could master this tendency. Through coaching, he was able to move through the negative energy and gradually developed a technique for letting go of the past wrongs he felt had been done to him.

FAMOUS FACES · SELF-RELIANT
George W. Bush, Madeleine Albright and Prince Harry.

Chapter Eight: Lips

CONCISE / VERBOSE

Thin upper lip   Full upper lip
Concise   Verbose

The degree of conciseness is determined by the fullness or thinness of the upper lip. The thinner the lip, the more Concise a person is; the fuller the upper lip, the more Verbose. However, this trait may change due to environmental. If children have been constantly put down, or if they have been shown very little affection or lived in an abusive home, their lips become very thin over time. I often see this trait in both men and women who've had a very hard life or have been through a painful divorce that has left them physically and emotionally drained. When the mouth is both thin and small in comparison to the whole design of the face, it may indicate extreme introversion or bottled-up feelings.

In California, they have a law called "three strikes, you're out," where a third felony conviction automatically sends you to prison for life. This happened to a man whose third crime was to steal a bicycle. When first interviewed by the television news program "60 Minutes," his lips were full; a year later he was interviewed again, and his lips had become so thin that they had practically disappeared.

Individuals who have thin lips are generally more concise; at times they may be perceived as being very terse and to the point.

Concise individuals dislike repetitious conversation; when the conversation gets too drawn out, they just turn it off in their head. During the 2000 United States presidential debates, Al Gore came across as very wordy, whereas George Bush was more concise and to the point. The advantage of concise people is that they can give clear, precise and easy-to-follow directions.

Concise persons may speak very rapidly and at length, particularly when they are nervous or are passionate about the topic they are talking about. Many writers with this trait have shared that they have a hard time filling up the pages; they say what they have to say in just a few words.

I WAS BEING INTERVIEWED BY ONE OF THE LOCAL TELEVISION NETWORKS AND THEY ASKED ME TO INVITE ANOTHER PERSON WHO WAS AN EXPERIENCED FACE READER TO JOIN ME ON THE PROGRAM. THE FACE READER I INVITED WAS DON, A THIN-LIPPED GENTLEMAN. AT THE TIME, THE THOUGHT FLASHED THROUGH MY MIND THAT I SHOULD REMIND HIM TO BE MORE EXPRESSIVE DURING THE INTERVIEW. WHEN QUESTIONED BY THE HOST, HIS RESPONSE WAS VERY BRIEF AND TO THE POINT. THE HOSTESS FOUND THE INTERVIEW SOMEWHAT CHALLENGING. ABOUT A WEEK LATER DON CALLED ME TO APOLOGIZE FOR BEING SO UNENGAGING ON THE SHOW.

This is one of the few physical features that can change without cosmetic surgery. Thin-lipped people could be verbose personalities who've bottled up their feelings due to their conditioning.

If you are sitting with a group of people and you notice one person is being very quiet, ask that person some open-ended questions; invite his or her opinion. Some High Concise people may be perceived as dull because they tend to be so quiet in social situations. They have lots to say, but they just need to be encouraged. Once you open them up, they will talk at length about what they love to work on, or offer some new insight to the conversation.

If you are a High Concise person, try to embellish your conversation – fill in with more detail than you would normally. If the person with whom you are meeting starts to talk at length, ask specific questions. Convey that you want to get directly to the point such by saying something like, "Could you sum it up in just a few words?" Try to be patient with people who are more expressive, and listen closely to the content of the conversation. You are creating a bond by acknowledging the other person's needs. Be more open to expressing your feelings with people who are close to you; they cannot second-guess how you feel towards them or what is going on for you.

A couple who were on the verge of divorce decided to have their personality profiles done. During the consultation, it was revealed that the husband, who had both a thinner upper and lower lip, truly cared about his wife but had a hard time expressing his feelings to her. The last thing he wanted was a divorce. The consultant stood behind the husband and expressed to his wife, for him, how he truly felt about her. Her response was, "I didn't know you cared; you never told me." Their charts revealed many of the challenges the couple had been experiencing and demonstrated how different each of them were. Now they had a tangible tool to work with and a way to appreciate each other's differences. It was the turning point in their marriage. Today they continue to have a closer relationship and understanding of each other.

A British man named Nigel went to visit his young daughter, accompanied by a friend who asked him, "Why don't you give her a hug and show her that you care?" His response was, "I'm here, aren't I?" He thought his presence was sufficient show of affection.

I asked Nigel about his childhood. His response was that he felt his parents never really wanted him. He did not recall his mother ever expressing her feelings towards him and seldom gave him a hug. His father was in the army and certainly no feelings were encouraged there. The thin upper lip is an observable trait in many English men. They are told to be tough from birth and are not encouraged to express their feelings. It's not "proper."

The next time you take the Underground in London, look around you and notice the significant number of men with very thin upper and lower lips. It leaves me feeling very sad for them. English people tend to bottle up their feelings. I think the day that Princess Diana died, the sadness brought out many of the feelings in their own lives. Her funeral made it safe to let them go.

Beware if you ask Verbose people for directions, because they'll give you the complete tour. Ask them how their day was and they'll give you every little detail. People with fuller lips have a natural ability to talk, and it takes very little effort to start up and continue a conversation. Verbose individuals spontaneously add more interest to what is being said. It has been known for them to talk until the wee hours of the morning, especially if their companion also has full lips.

If you find yourself at the airport waiting for a delayed flight, look for someone with full lips to talk to; they will keep you thoroughly entertained. Time will fly by.

If you work with or meet someone who tends to be very verbose, ask them questions that elicit a "yes" or "no" response. Or premise your questions by saying, "Could you briefly describe the situation?" Or look at your watch – that will indicate you've only so much time otherwise you might be spending hours with them.

The positive aspect of the Verbose trait is that these people can speak at length when required, e.g., as an after-dinner speaker or a children's story teller. Their speech is more colorful and flowing and adds interest to the story or speech. They need to be aware of repetition or listeners may become quickly bored. Many people who have African heritage tend to have fuller lips, and they are very expressive. However, we will also find some people within the culture will have thinner lips – for example, Reverend Jesse Jackson. The fullness of the lips is determined by comparing the size of the lips to the overall size of the face. It is not determined by comparing the size to other people's lips.

If you are more verbose, be aware when you are speaking at length or you may lose the attention of the person with whom you are talking. Organize your thoughts before speaking. In a job interview, you could easily talk yourself into or out of a job. Give yourself some space to think things through. If you have this trait, and find yourself being interviewed on radio or television, make sure you keep your response brief and to the point. Airtime is expensive.

Be aware of long, drawn-out conversations; check to see if the other person is still paying attention. After such a conversation, the thin-lipped person may have felt they have wasted precious time. They dislike conversation for the sake of itself. So, all you folks who love to talk, look for the signals, and keep it short and to the point when needed.

FAMOUS FACES · VERBOSE

Mick Jagger, Martha Stewart, Julia Roberts and Oprah Winfrey.

GENEROUS

FULL LOWER LIP
Very generous of their time and money

The fuller the lower lip in comparison to the size of the person's face, the more generous he or she is. Individuals with this trait will give before being asked. They will give more than is required; this includes time, money and possessions. They will give without hesitation when they see there is a greater need by others.

During the Christmas season, Ann was out on a present-buying spree in downtown San Francisco. She was approached by a homeless person who was begging for money. Her first response was to not give the person anything. Then she thought, "Well, it's Christmas. Give him some money. It might bring a few moments of pleasure to this person." Looking through her purse, she only found large bills. "Well, why not?" she thought to herself.

The man was surprised at her generous donation. A month later she found herself in the same area, and who should be there but this man. She hastily retreated to the store; however, the homeless man spoke to Ann's husband, asking him to personally extend his gratitude to her. He said that he had used the money she gave him to set up a street vending business.

The extremely generous person will buy a round of drinks for everyone when he/she has hardly enough money for their bare necessities. During the holiday season he will give elaborate gifts to all of his friends and family when he should really be paying the bills. Whereas the person who has the opposite of this trait will see this giving as a complete waste of money and see no point in it. One client stated that automatic giving is almost obsessive for her to the point where she neglects her family. She never saves, because she sees no point. Save it for what?

People who score high on this trait have a tendency to over extend themselves both in terms of their time and their money. They take on more than they can handle. While they give automatically, they often find it hard to receive gifts from others, and it will appear that they are not open to receiving.

If you are a generous individual, learn when to say "no" before over extending yourself, and only give what you can reasonably afford, whether it is time or possessions. Individuals who have this trait with a combination of High Impulsiveness (protruding lips), and Low Acquisitiveness (ears flat against the head), may give away everything they own.

If you have the Generous trait, allow others the pleasure of giving to you. Knowing the pleasure you receive from the act of giving to others allows you to see how others would appreciate an opportunity to be grateful and appreciative towards you. When you refuse gifts, or show a lack of enthusiasm, it can deeply hurt the giver's feelings and they can feel rejected. Just imagine how you'd feel if someone rejected your generosity.

Sometimes individuals with thin lips feel the act of giving is rather frivolous and unnecessary. This was the case with a newly married couple. Pat's husband seldom gave her any gifts other than for her birthday. I suggested that he surprise her with a bunch of flowers. A few weeks later Pat called up feeling very excited for she had found a rose from her husband on her computer screen. Later he gave her a bunch of real red roses. Her husband realized how much this meant to Pat.

If you are less giving, learn to give to others without any strings attached. Give more of yourself in personal relationships and spend more time helping others who would benefit from your assistance. Express your feelings more. Surprise your significant other with a bouquet of flowers or a favorite bottle of wine. Open up your feelings to your children and express how much you care about them. Make sure you are available to them.

FAMOUS FACES · GENEROUS

Jimmy Carter, Al Gore, Jennifer Aniston and Richard Branson.

TAKING THINGS PERSONALLY

SHORT PHILTRUM
Takes criticism very personally

The tendency to "take things personally" – a phrase created by Jones – is determined by the length of the philtrum (the distance from the top of the lip to the base of the nose in comparison to the length of the face). The shorter the philtrum, the stronger that desire is for individuals to look good. He or she is very aware of their appearance. This trait also indicates these individuals will take criticism very personally. They like to look good and act in a socially acceptable way, paying attention to the rules of etiquette and fashion. They want to look right for every occasion. They are very conscious about any unsightly scars or bruises on their face; this will really bother them. At the first signs of sagging and lines in their faces, they will spend huge amounts of money to get rid of the imperfections. In the extreme, they can almost be obsessive about their appearance.

Individuals with this trait enjoy clothes and may have an extensive wardrobe. They have a natural ability for creating attractive clothing combinations. This trait is often seen in designers, personal shoppers and sales assistants in clothing or cosmetic departments.

Individuals with this trait may appear to be extremely vain and can't go by a mirror without checking their appearance.

Such was the case of a young man in a hotel lobby. He kept checking himself in the glass pictures, brushing his hands through his hair many times over. Not that it changed his appearance; it was probably a reassurance that his image was still intact since checking it a few minutes ago.

Individuals with this trait are extremely image conscious. They go to great pains to look good, appear successful, and only want to put their best foot forward. They fear criticism so much that they become fanatics about how they come across to others.

Individuals who have this trait are also very sensitive to criticism. Sharon sees criticism of her work as her being a failure. She feels completely destroyed and will wake up in the night worrying about it. When criticized, she "goes into an emotional hole" and feels "as small as a pea." As you may have guessed, she also has Low tolerance (close-set eyes). She thinks people must hate her when something is not done on time. She took criticism to mean that she was absolute failure and no one liked her. She would bend any even slightly negative comments to the point of being completely out of context. After a while she would begin to believe them. Her close-set eyes tended to keep her focused to the point where the problem became bigger than life. If you have this trait, try not to take things so personally. Clear up any miscommunication right away and be ready to talk about what was said that hurt your feelings. Be open to hearing and listening to the other person's response.

John said he takes criticism personally and has a difficult time with it to the point where it paralyzes him. He gets the most criticism about his writing. This created a block for him when he was a young child. During the times when his parents were at each other's throats, he would escape to his room and write stories. Both his parents and teachers heavily criticized his writing. They told him he was wasting his time. You'll be glad to hear he never gave up his dream. After some years he became a very successful writer. If you know of a child or adult who has an interest in writing, support them with your encouragement. Who knows, they could become a successful writer or journalist.

Geoffrey Thompson, author of *The Great Escape*, had always wanted to become a writer. When he was a child, he was never given the support or encouragement to follow his dream. It wasn't until later that his dream became a reality. He is now the author of many books and a consultant to film directors.

CAREERS

Fashion designers, models, personal shoppers, color consultants, and aestheticians.

FAMOUS FACES · TAKES THINGS PERSONALLY

Leonardo DiCaprio, Elizabeth Hurley, Jennifer Aniston and Brad Pitt.

DRY SENSE OF HUMOR

LONG PHILTRUM

Dry sense of humor

This trait is determined by a long space from the top of the lip to the base of the nose. In stark contrast to the Takes Things Personally, an individual with the Dry Humor trait will take criticism with a grain of salt. Criticism tends to run off them just like water off a duck's back. They will appear to be impervious to other people's feelings. They have a very dry sense of humor; not everyone gets their jokes. At times, they can unintentionally come across as being very sarcastic.

Dry humor may be amusing to some people but can have devastating effects on others, especially when the remarks are cutting and sarcastic. This is a challenging trait to have because, when out of control, it can shatter relationships. A man went to visit his parents whom he hadn't seen for some time. One of his parents immediately made a sarcastic remark about his appearance. Throughout his stay, there were repeated incidents of cutting remarks directed toward him, to the point where he just wanted to leave. If you have this trait, be more aware of the effect this has on other people, particularly those with fine hair and a short philtrum (Takes Things Personally). It can leave them devastated.

Such was the case with a member of my family who has this trait. I greeted him with a big hug; his arms remained down by his side. I said to him, "Come on…. you can give me a hug." His sarcastic response was, "Oh, I'd never be able to get my arms around you," which he said with a smirk. In the kindest tone I could muster, I said, "I am sure you did not intend to be offensive. However, some people could be really hurt by that remark. You really need to be more sensitive to other people's feelings." Later on that week he did compliment me. To me this demonstrated he was sorry about the remark. If something is said that hurts your feelings, clear it up right away in a manner that will bring positive results rather than it ending up in a shouting match or resentment.

It's a lot easier for Dry Humor people to be sarcastic to their family. One husband said he was the target of his wife's sarcasm. To her, it was not a big deal. So why was he overreacting to her comments? She has coarse hair (Less Sensitive) and a dry humor, so things do not get to her quite as quickly. Her husband tried to explain how her remarks embarrassed him in front of people. Her response was, "It didn't embarrass me."

People who have the Dry Humor trait are more concerned with getting the job done, rather than how they look. When they dress in the morning, they would much rather put on comfortable clothes than get all dressed up. They are less interested in the current clothing trends. They are the personal shoppers' dream clients because there is so much improvement that can be achieved. These individuals get so wrapped up in what they're doing that how they look is the last thing on their mind.

When shopping for clothes, hire a personal shopper; this will save you time and money in the long run. In addition, you will know that you'll always look good without having to work at it. Hiring someone to help you will make the shopping experience an enjoyable one rather than one of necessity. This more casual approach to shopping is modified when the skin seems to be very tight on the frame of the face. These people enjoy dressing well but not to the point of being vain.

FAMOUS FACES · DRY SENSE OF HUMOR

David Letterman, George Burns, William Hague, George W. Bush, and Colin Powell.

IMPULSIVENESS

PROTRUDING LIPS

Says and acts without thought

A person's impulsiveness can be gauged from the side profile and is indicated by how much the lips protrude past the ridge of the nose near the center of the eyebrows. Take a pencil and line up with the ridge of the nose, making sure the head is level. When looking at the profile of the face, do the lips project forward or recede? If the lips protrude, this indicates the person is very impulsive. Highly impulsive individuals will say and do things in the moment that they may regret later. They act without thinking, which can often get them into trouble.

Those with High Impulsiveness tend to interrupt conversations and may bring up something from out of the blue. They often speak without thinking about the impact their words will have on others. Sometimes they are seen as "knee jerk" parties and can be especially thoughtless if they are drinking alcohol. These are also the impulsive spenders. They should ask themselves first if they really need to purchase the item or invest in the stock market. This trait, along with Objective Thinking (sloped-back forehead) is a quality needed for people whose career relies on a quick response.

Impulsive individuals are very enthusiastic about life. If you try to caution them they will not take it very kindly. If their friends are not quite so spontaneous they will see them as "wet blankets."

Low Impulsive people tend to be more calculated in thought and action. They are more deliberate and not prone to quick or impetuous decisions. People with Low Impulsiveness and Sequential Thinking will take time to consider a major buying decision. Do not try to rush these people into making a purchase. Give them some space to think through their decision.

If you are a very impulsive, look before you leap or you may regret your decision. Learn not to interrupt a conversation. Pay attention to what is being said, and allow the other person to complete their comment or response. Count to ten before you say anything and leave more of your thoughts unspoken.

If you tend to be less impulsive, do something spontaneous for once and see how it feels.

CAREERS

High Impulsiveness: paramedics, fire fighters, public speakers, radio and TV broadcasters, auctioneers, interpreters and sales people.

FAMOUS FACES · IMPULSIVE

Tony Blair, Bill Gates, tennis players Serena and Venus Williams.

YOU CAN READ A FACE LIKE A BOOK

OPTIMISM / PESSIMISM

UPTURNED MOUTH	DOWNTURNED MOUTH
Optimistic	Pessimistic

Pessimism is a trait recognizable by the downward turn of the outer corners of the mouth. This is another environmental trait that develops over time by the muscles being constantly pulled down at the corners of the mouth. It usually reflects the inner negative chatter that goes on in the pessimist's head. This trait is mostly seen in adults where life's circumstances have taken a toll on their faces. This tendency is most noticeable in older people.

I once met a business owner whose mouth was turned down at one corner. Her business was going well, but she was afraid she would not be able to fill the orders. When no orders were coming in, she thought the business was probably going to fail. Her business was, in fact, quite successful. No matter how much the sun was shining on her that day there was always a storm ready to come in.

Pessimists look at the dark side of life and are hard to please. Their thoughts immediately go to what is not working or they look at the worst-case scenario. With some coaching, they can change.

If you are Pessimistic, ask yourself what it would be like to be around people who are constantly negative. How would you feel? Would you want to seek out their company? What would you advise them? What are the steps you can take now to look at the more positive side of life? When you find yourself going into negative self-talk, close your eyes and simply empty out your thoughts. Or if you find yourself driving your car and the thoughts are pouring into your head, simply decide not to go there. Once you practice ways to let go, you will be able to do it instantly.

It is not enough to simply "let go" of negative thoughts – the mind abhors a vacuum. One has to learn to replace the emptiness with positive thoughts or the mind simply reverts to negativity.

Individuals with both Pessimism and High Critical traits can be very hard on themselves, so much so that after a while they wear themselves down and others with them. If this trait is combined with Backward Balance (more head in back of ears), a person will tend to bring up the negative things that happened in the past over and over again. This will further contribute to the pessimism, reinforcing an already tainted attitude – "This is the way it has always been and always will be."

CHILDREN

We do not see this trait in children; they are usually fairly positive by nature.

CHAPTER NINE: THE JAW

AUTHORITATIVE

WIDE JAW

Likes to be in charge

The wider the jaw, the more authoritative the person will sound and appear. Hillary Clinton is a good example of someone with this feature. She also has a very wide face (High Self-Confidence) that adds to her authoritative appearance. A narrow jaw line is less authoritative. George W. Bush has a narrow jaw. He certainly appears less authoritative when he is standing next to Bill Clinton, Colin Powell or Tony Blair. He does not carry the air of someone confident in what he is doing.

The wide jaw gives resonance to the voice and the person will come across as being very strong and powerful. These highly authoritative individuals have a natural tendency to take charge. It is hard for them to take a back seat, especially when others hesitate. When they see other people fumbling or showing hesitation, in their viewpoint that individual is not really trying. There are times when they can come across as being very opinionated.

When the High Authoritative individuals step into a room, they do not have to say a word. They have a strong presence and they look as if they are in charge. This air of authority is heightened if the person also has a wide face. These individuals can be quite intimidating. This can be a distinct asset at times when strong leadership is needed. They command respect, like to be "In charge," and are very decisive in the way they speak. The minute these individuals feel threatened, they become tense and their voices become louder, particularly if they have coarse hair. High Authoritative individuals need to cultivate a warmer tone in their voice.

Women who have this trait should avoid using strong colors such as navy, black, royal blue and bright red when in a general meeting with their business associates or department. Cheryl was the head of her department. She would often wear strong colors when attending a department meeting. The employees who reported to her found her very intimidating and would remain silent in the meeting rather than express their concerns. Once advice was given to her to use softer colors, everyone relaxed and a lot more was accomplished. Fellow employees did not feel as threatened.

When working with people who have this trait, do not accept their apparent "take charge" attitude when they are not actually in charge. Understand that this can be their style of expression and their natural way of communicating. If you have this trait, think about how you may be sounding to others who are less authoritative. Develop an awareness of how you are communicating with them, soften your voice and try not to be too pushy. Think of a way to soften your approach that will produce a more positive outcome. If you come across as being more authoritative, use this trait to your advantage when needed; back off when appropriate. If you come across as being too authoritative or aggressive it will put people off. This could set up hostility and work against you when the support from others is needed.

People with narrow jaws are not very assertive. If they are highly competitive, forceful and progressive, this kind of energy is more aggressive rather than authoritative.

If you have a narrow jaw line (Less Authoritative) and fine hair, cultivate a stronger and more decisive tone, especially when interacting with people who have wider faces and jaws. Wear deeper but neutral colors such as navy, black, forest green, burgundy or dark purple. These more formal colors will support your verbal and visual message. Cultivate a stronger voice when working in a situation that requires you to be more authoritative. Be gently assertive to individuals who are exhibiting authoritative behavior; let them know you intend to be in charge.

RELATIONSHIPS

If you come across as being too aggressive in relationships, it may smother the other person's growth. Let the other person have their say, too. If your children are very aggressive, it might be a good idea to remind them how this works against them.

FAMOUS FACES · LOW AUTHORITATIVE

George W. Bush, Tom Hanks, and Jennifer Aniston.

FAMOUS FACES · HIGH AUTHORITATIVE

Hillary Clinton, John Wayne, Ted Kennedy, and Cheri Blair.

AUTOMATIC RESISTANCE

POINTED CHIN

Very stubborn

People whose jaws look wedge-shaped (pointed chin), automatically resist when they are told what to do. They will put up a strong resistance and automatically say "no," when they feel any hint of pressure. The more they are pushed, the more they will dig in their heels and refuse to budge. Working with people who have this trait will make you feel like you're pushing against a brick wall. They can be extremely stubborn. However, they can be easily persuaded if you give them the reasons why you need them to do something. An explanation works far better than pressure.

When Karen is told what to do, she will appear to be cooperating on the outside but inside she is digging her heels in and rebelling. Push her too far and the flag will go up, indicating a very strong "no." Just when everything appears to be okay is when the Automatic Resistant individual explodes. Karen found that when she was feeling stressed out at work, walking or yoga and Tai Chi really helped to balance her day. Without this activity, she said, she would be an emotional wreck.

On the outside, Automatic Resistant individuals appear to be handling the pressure much better than most. However, they keep things bottled up inside them while seemingly handling a situation. This may eventually manifest itself through ulcers, shingles or break out in a facial rash. This prolonged stress can be seen in the eyes. When the white of the eye is showing underneath one of the irises, this will indicate the beginning stages of stress. If the whites are showing under both eyes, the stress is prolonged. If you are a personal coach, and your client has these signs, you might want to first deal with the stress or suggest they seek some help in dealing with whatever is going on in their life. Otherwise, it's just piling more stuff on them.

If you have this trait, rather than automatically saying "no" to everything, try coming back with, "Let me get back to you on that" or, "I'll think it over." This will avoid much of the frustration experienced by the other person and it keeps the communication open. Ask yourself what you are gaining by being stubborn without justification. What is it that you are resisting? Are you being reasonable, and is your resistance based on principle or feelings? If you find yourself under this kind of pressure, think of something you could do now to relieve the tension, such as go for a walk by the water, listen to a piece of music, or any activity that will help you relax.

CHILDREN

When stubbornness is a problem in a young child, explain the reasons why you want them to do something rather than saying, "You have to, that's why." When you give children and adults motivating reasons, they will come around.

FAMOUS FACES · AUTOMATIC RESISTANT

Winston Churchill, Oprah Winfrey, and Mel Gibson.

PUGNACITY

SQUARE CHIN

The love of debate

Pugnacity is determined by the squareness of the chin. Good examples of people with this trait would be David Letterman, John Major and Deepak Chopra, who all have very square chins. Individuals with this trait love to get into good meaty discussions. They will fight for what they believe in, whether it is a favorite cause or social justice. These are the people who never give up; they have a "fighting spirit." They do well in debate or mediation. They are good at presenting both sides of a situation.

The Pugnacity trait indicates the person physically and verbally responds to situations in the moment. A friend and I visited one of the local court sessions in England and, after listening to several cases being heard, we decided to leave. As we exited the courtroom, a policewoman who immediately wanted to know what we had been doing in court followed us out. My Pugnacious companion lashed out at her and told her in no uncertain terms that, as English citizens, we had every right to be there. His response was much stronger and more confrontational that was necessary or appropriate. I spoke to my friend afterward and, over time, he has learned to gain control over this automatic response. Modifying a behavioral tendency does not happen overnight. It takes a strong, consistent desire to change the behavior.

Another behavior that is also related to individuals with the Pugnacity trait is that they will "appear" to be going along with the situation; however, they may not feel that way inside. Later they may well pull out of their commitment because the project or situation did not work out as they hoped. This can be confusing to people they work with, who probably thought all was well. If you have this trait, let the other people involved know up front what your expectations are, rather than going along with the situation.

Maria was always ready to jump in with her opinion, whether it was solicited or not. She liked to get involved with the discussion and say what she wanted to say. She liked to set the story and the facts right. Growing up with six brothers, her interest in expressing her opinions had been put aside on the back burner. Now, as an adult, she loves to get together with friends and have a good debate. She told me that they have all agreed not to agree. In her work, she helps couples resolve conflicts, something she really enjoys.

Sometimes people with the Pugnacity trait go out of their way to pick a fight. If you have this trait, keep in mind that fighting is not the solution; you may frighten someone or end up doing some physical abuse. If a person also has the Intense Feelings trait (long thumb), he or she should be aware that it is particularly important to master this trait combination. Think of another way to handle the situation so that the outcome is not so aggressive. If you are with someone who displays this aggressive behavior, you might suggest in a quiet tone that he or she talk about the situation before it gets out of hand.

Many people I have talked to say they found that exercising, running, boxing, working out at a gym or engaging in any activity that gives them a physical outlet really helped to channel this energy.

The French actor Gérard Depardieu once stated in an interview that if he had not taken up acting, he might have ended up in prison. His chin is certainly very square.

CHILDREN

In children this trait may be easier to observe in their behavior rather than by the physical feature. If one of the parents has this trait, then the chances are good that the child will inherit similar behavior. If this is a tendency in your child then get her into sports or any activity where she can channel her energy.

CAREERS

Trial lawyers, mediators, rugby players, boxers, and male gymnasts.

FAMOUS FACES · PUGNACITY

John Cleese, David Letterman, Gérard Depardieu and Tony Blair.

TENACITY

PROTRUDING CHIN

Very tenacious

Tenacity is indicated by the amount of chin protruding forward when viewed from the side. The more the chin protrudes forward, the more tenacious the person is; Jay Leno is a good example of a highly tenacious person. A receding chin will indicate the person is Low Tenacious, and tends to let go of situations too quickly.

Once Tenacious individuals get their teeth into a project or relationship, they hang on to the bitter end. They have a tendency to hold on to whatever it is they are doing, right or wrong. They can take commitment to a relationship, a job or anything else to extreme levels, even when it might be against their best interests. They need to learn to stop and reassess a situation when it isn't working for them, and either drop the project or take a different approach. They need to learn when it's time to let go, rather than hanging on, hoping things will work out.

If you have this High Tenacious trait, hang on for the right reasons, but do not go down with the ship. Before starting a new project or venture, set reasonable goals. Define what you really want to happen before tackling the problem. Then you will know whether or not to hang on, and why. Learn to let go, if what you are doing does not work into your long-term plans.

The Low Tenacious person (receding chin) does not "Hang on for the sake of hanging on." They are more willing to let go of a situation when it isn't useful. This makes them easier to work with. However, when the pressure is on, they may well walk off the job.

This lack of tenacity could also apply to letting go of relationships too soon. Low Tenacious people can find commitment too burdensome and might bail out if the going gets tough at all.

If you have this trait, ask yourself whether you are letting go too soon. What if you were to hang in there just a little longer? Set your goals; this will help you to get through the times when you just want to give up. Goals will remind you why you are taking the task on and will give you something to focus on. When you are ready to back off, stop and review your goals. If you are still going in the right direction, you might want to hang in there for a while longer.

FAMOUS FACES · HIGH TENACITY

The Duchess of York, Vanessa Redgrave, John Cleese, and Jay Leno.

PHYSICAL MOTIVE

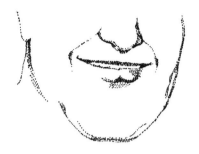

DISTANCE FROM BASE OF NOSE TO CHIN
Restless – The need to be on the go

Physical Motive can be assessed by measuring the length of the face from the base of the chin to the base of the nose. This measurement is compared with the entire length of the face. The longer the space, the more restless this person will be. Individuals with this trait are constantly on the go, physically active doing something. The shorter this space is, the more the person will use their mind to sort things out rather than physically responding to situations. The Physical Motive person will leap to action, whereas the person who has the opposite trait will sit and think about the situation for a moment.

Physical Motive individuals are constantly on the move; they have an enormous amount of stamina and, seemingly, an endless supply of energy. They can keep going when others have already given up. Individuals with this trait have to be constantly doing something; just sitting and watching television is quite challenging, particularly if they also have short legs (remember that similar restlessness came up in the section on short-legged people). It's very hard for these individuals to relax. There will be a part of them that will want to get up and do something more constructive. One woman expressed her frustration that her husband was constantly on the go; he never seemed to take the time and sit with her in the evenings. Her father-in-law was the same way. It was one of her biggest complaints.

Next time you are watching a soccer, rugby or football game notice how many of the players have high physical motive (long lower face). Many boxers and wrestlers have this trait, along with square chins.

Mark has short legs and is a Physical Motive individual who has a desk job. He says he lives a large portion of his life feeling like an animal in a cage. Working out at a gym gives him an outlet for his frustrations; it releases the boredom and gives him more energy. This greatly improves his relationship with his family because he doesn't take his frustrations out on them.

Sally had a trait combination of High Tolerance (wide-set eyes) and High Physical Motive (long lower face). She found it very difficult to focus during her earlier years in school. She found sitting still for long periods of time very difficult, and still finds it hard today. When she exercises the problem goes away; the exercise brings balance to her day.

I happen to have this High Restless trait. My husband tells me I need to hike a mountain each day, maybe even two mountains. In order to survive sitting still on a long airline flight, I get up extra early and go for a brisk walk. I never take the moving walkways at the airport. This gives me some added exercise before boarding the plane. If you have this trait, make sure you get up during the flight, move around and stretch your legs.

If you find you're getting irritable or restless, take time out and go for a brisk walk. You will be able to focus better on your work and your efforts will be far more productive.

Relationships

People who score high on Physical Motive like to be where the action is, and like to be physically active. It is harder for them to slow down and relax. They have so much energy that sometimes they do not know what to do with themselves. If the other person within the relationship has the opposite trait, he or she may find it difficult to keep up with their partner.

Children

Children who score high on this trait have boundless energy. This energy needs to be channeled into activities such as soccer, tennis, dancing or gymnastics.

It was Halloween and the children were in the neighborhood knocking on the door and calling out, "Trick or Treat." One young man, upon hearing that I was English, started to sing, "I am a Londoner, yes, I am." In return I asked if he would like me to read his face and I proceeded to do so. I told him he would be good at sports, whereupon he asked which sport. I replied soccer. He was totally amazed. His friends then all requested a reading. As they turned around to walk down the path, they shouted out to their parents, "You'll never believe what this lady just told us." They will definitely remember that Halloween. The young man had all the traits of High Physical Motive (long lower face) and High Music Appreciation (rounded ears) plus Short Legs, Objective Thinking and Competitive.

Hobbies

Working out at a gym, hiking, or any kind of sports.

Famous Faces · Physical Motive

David Beckham (who plays soccer for England), Sidney Poitier, Boris Yeltsin, Steffi Graf, and Nelson Mandela.

MENTAL MOTIVE

SHORT SPACE BETWEEN BASE OF CHIN AND NOSE
Stimulated by mental activity

People who have a shorter distance from the base of the chin to the base of the nose score high on Mental Motive. They are stimulated by mental challenges. Mental activity is as consuming to them as physical activity is to the physically motivated. They accomplish more through the mental process than through physical action. Without a mental challenge, they may become bored in their jobs. If they are also long-legged, it is very easy for these individuals to spend hours sitting reading a book, watching a video or television or simply just sitting and thinking about life in general. To others they appear to be "couch potatoes." Individuals with this trait need to make sure they include some physical activity on a regular basis. Anything physical is recommended, such as working out at a gym, bicycling, playing golf or swimming. Just as the High Physical person needs to take time out for mental activity, the High Mental Motive person need to take time out for exercise.

These High Mental Motive individuals spend a lot of time in their heads with their thoughts. They think things through. Mental activity can be as exhausting as any physical activity. They need to get out of their heads and have more fun. Jennifer, a client of mine with a short lower face, finds the mental activity to be very satisfying because she can keep herself company for hours and enjoys the thinking process. At times, however, it can work against her and she can become overly obsessive about what is not working in her life. There is a fine line between contemplative thought and mental obsessiveness concerning what she is upset about. Using meditation, she is able to work through her obsessive thoughts.

If you have this trait, make sure you balance your mental activity with physical needs. When you are involved with high physical activity for long periods, make sure you take time out to rest.

CAREERS

Research or university instructor.

HOBBIES

Chess, bridge or any activity that requires a lot of thought. For children, challenge their minds to keep them interested.

FAMOUS FACES · MENTAL MOTIVE

Madeleine Albright, John Grisham, Vladimir Putin, Diane Sawyer and Tom Hanks.

Chapter Ten: The Cheekbones

Adventurous

Cheekbones
The love of adventure

This trait of adventurousness is correlated with how much the cheekbones protrude from the sides and front of the face. Individuals with prominent cheekbones love adventure and need to have constant change in their daily lives. They want to be where things are happening, they get emotional excitement from new experiences and exploring new territories. Adventurous individuals enjoy variety in their day. In repetitive situations, they become quickly bored. People who love to travel and are eager to make changes are the discoverers and the explorers. Their challenge is boredom; they need change and have a great sense of adventure.

Susan felt extremely frustrated because her husband did not like to travel. He preferred to go fishing or just putter around in the garden, activities that she found very boring. It was suggested she find a group of people or a friend who would like to travel with her – people who shared her sense of adventure.

Meg is a High Adventurous woman in her seventies. After her husband died, she sold their home and bought a boat and camper. She now travels the harbors and canals of England and stays at one place until she feels ready to move on. She has no phone; the family waits for her to call them from time to time just to let them know where she is.

Alan, an international marketing representative for a large company, stated he was just short of having traveled two million air miles. I asked him if he ever got fed up with all the travel. His response was that he would hate a desk job, that he would be able to do it for a while but would need the opportunity for change.

Individuals with this trait may confuse their nomadic spirit with the need to be constantly on the move and changing residences. They are very adaptable to change and enjoy their nomadic life. This trait can be seen in many of the Romany Gypsies who adapted well to their lifestyle. I spoke to an author who had written a book about the Tribes of Iran and gave her what I thought would be a facial description of these people without actually seeing them. She said the facial characteristics described them exactly.

The Adventurous person will feel that others who are less adventurous are missing out on the excitement. She will feel restricted if her partner does not have the same enthusiasm for travel. If you are more adventurous, use your free time to travel or take up a hobby that gives you the variety you need. Keep in mind not everyone shares your enthusiasm for change. If this is an issue in your relationship, discuss how you can arrange time together to avoid the feeling of being tied to the home. This is a challenge for some people because they feel that a commitment to a permanent relationship will cramp their lifestyle and curtail their freedom.

The Low Adventurous individual (no prominent cheekbones) may appear to be a "stick in the mud" to some people. These individuals are more content to stay at home. They do not feel the need to travel to distant places. They enjoy exploring the areas that are close to home. To the more adventurous person this will seem like a very dull life.

CHILDREN

Children who have this Adventurous trait need constant change and excitement. If this is not satisfied, they may get into mischief just for the thrill it provides, especially if they also have long ring fingers (High Risk Taking). Make sure their days include a variety of activities.

CAREERS

Flight attendants (notice the next time you fly how many attendants have this trait), travel agents, tour guides, international marketing or sales.

FAMOUS FACES · HIGH ADVENTUROUS

Hillary Clinton, J.K. Rowling, Steffi Graf, and Raquel Welch.

CHAPTER ELEVEN: THE EARS

MUSIC APPRECIATION

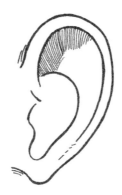

ROUNDED OUTER EDGE OF EAR
Music appreciation

This trait is determined by the roundness of the outer perimeter of the ear. The more rounded the ear, the greater the sensitivity to sound and rhythm. The structure of the ear is simply a channel for "intake of sound." The more rounded the structure, the greater accuracy and reception of sound. Sound has great power to evoke feelings and emotions. For some people, music is enjoyable to listen to but is not a high priority. To others, the sound of a bell, the sound of the wind, the sound of the waves can be music to the ears.

The High Music trait is a great asset to the individual who works in sound engineering or tunes musical instruments. If she also has Aesthetic Appreciation (straight eyebrows) this will heighten her sensual response to music. Individuals with this trait cluster are attuned to the vibration and how the music flows. Andrew Lloyd Weber, the composer of the musical *Cats*, is a good example of the following cluster of Aesthetic Appreciation (straight eyebrows),

Music Appreciation, Design Appreciation (inverted V on eyebrow) and drama (flared eyebrows)

The Aesthetic person "feels" music rather than just hearing it. Music becomes a part of his total sense of expression. Sometimes the "ear for music" may not be present and still the individual will be a professional or serious musician. Such musicians aim to create feeling. When the inner helix of the ear is also completely rounded, this indicates the individual has good pitch. If the ear is cupped out this will heighten her appreciation. She catches every sound. When this trait is combined with Critical Perception (outer corners of eyes lower than inner corners) will make a great music critic.

When the trait of Music Appreciation is combined with fine hair (sensitivity), you'll have a connoisseur of music. Music for him is food for the soul. The fine-haired person will enjoy softer music, while the coarse-haired individual will turn up the sound. It does not reflect musical preference such as classic versus rock, just the quality of the sound.

Rounded ears are noticeable in many professional soccer/football and tennis players. While I was at Heathrow airport there was a team of young football/soccer players waiting to board a plane. Without exception, they all had extremely rounded ears and short to medium legs. I would think having this Music Appreciation trait is an advantage since we may observe there is a smoother transition in their movements. Music Appreciation would certainly be an asset for ice skating or dancing. They feel and express the music they hear, more than individuals who do not have this trait.

Jean, a student in my class in England, was traveling on the train to London. There was standing room only. As she looked at the ears of the man standing next to her, she noticed he had the very trait we discussed in class the previous day. She plucked up courage and gave him a brief explanation of the class she was taking and then asked him if he played a musical instrument. He was somewhat amazed and responded with "Yes, I did as a teenager," whereupon she encouraged him to take it up again and suggested he would feel more balanced in life if he were to do so. Nothing more was said until they got off the train. He turned around and said, "I've been giving some thought about what you suggested. I've decided to take up playing my clarinet again. Thank you." Jean was thrilled. This wasn't a wild guess; the observation was made based on years of research. I know of no other system that can access information so quickly and accurately without lengthy tests or questioning.

When this trait is combined with vocal lines (two lines on the neck that run across the vocal cords), this enhances the singer's performance.

FAMOUS FACES · MUSIC APPRECIATION

Luciano Pavarotti, Sarah Brightman, and Andrea Bocelli.

PIONEERING TREND

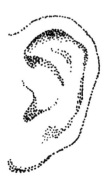

STRAIGHT OUTER EDGE OF EAR
The Pioneer

The Pioneering trait is indicated by the straightness of the outside rim (helix) of the ear. Individuals with this trait will do better working for themselves. They are the pioneers of new ideas and like being on the leading edge of new technology. They like to explore new territory and start new projects. These are the visionaries who have a burning desire to be the first to venture into a new field. They feel frustrated working for other people because it curtails their independent spirit. Individuals who do not have this trait enjoy working for other people.

The greatest challenge for these High Pioneering people is to stay focused and not get too impatient when things don't happen quickly enough for them. They crave to go beyond the horizon, to find out what's next or new and different. They want "to tread where no one else has trod before."

When this trait is combined with the ski jump nose (Ministrative), these individuals will want to work for themselves. The challenge will be handling the financial side. Once they master the business side or hire someone in that department, they can be successful.

A young man who sets up dance events struggled for a long time to make his business financially successful. His focus was creating a great space for people to dance and socialize without the usual bar scene. The concept worked and the events became very popular; however, there was a problem on the financial side. Generating cash flow and a reliable profit was a real struggle. The thought of working for someone else for a secure paycheck was not appealing to him. He did not want to give up his dream, but the business did not generate the cash flow needed to support his family. He had to decide whether to continue this as a sideline or simply acknowledge he had fun giving the idea a run for its money. His Tenaciousness (protruding chin) helped him to continue when others might well have given up.

If an individual with this trait also has the trait cluster of Ministrative (ski jump nose), High Generosity (large lower lip), and Low Acquisitiveness (ears laid back against their head), they need to have a partner or hire someone to handle the financial side of the business.

FAMOUS FACES · PIONEERING
   Richard Gere

GROWING TREND

LARGE EAR LOBE
Personal growth

Individuals with large ear lobes are naturally inclined to support others in their personal growth. This trait also indicates an interest in planting and maintaining living things. Individuals with the trait combination of Construction (square forehead) and Growing Trend (large ear lobes) will put the garden in but will want someone else to maintain it. The same with indoor plants. It will take a greater sustained effort for them to maintain and water the plants. In contrast, an individual with an oval forehead (Conservation) will love to plant the garden and will enjoy maintaining it on a regular basis. Add coarse hair to this cluster and you will have a person who loves to be in the outdoors. For many people, gardening is their way of escape from the daily stress of life.

Ear lobes increase in size as people get older. The chances are the Growing Trend trait was well developed in their earlier years.

CAREERS
Forest rangers, geologists, biologists, archaeologists, gardeners, psychologists, personal coaches, or environmental activists.

IDEALISTIC

LOW SET EARS (EAR OPENING IS LOWER THAN NOSTRIL)
Head in the clouds – high standards

The feature that indicates idealism is the placement of the ears. If the ears are low set, below the level of the nostrils, the individual is Idealistic. When the ears are higher than the level of the nostrils this will indicate he/she is more practical or realistic.

Idealism indicates the depth of feeling that people have about the ideals and standards they have chosen for themselves. It does not indicate what their ideals or standards are but rather how dedicated they will be to them. The Idealistic person has very high standards, and will seek perfection in herself and others. Idealistic people can be very demanding. They are very disappointed when reality is different from what they think it should be.

Once Idealistic individuals completely set their focus on something, they tend to lose sight of what is going on around them. Combine this trait, with Low Tolerance (close eyes), High Sensitive (fine hair), narrow face and Philosophical tendencies (gaps between the fingers), identifies individuals who could really get lost in their dreams. They may become so fanatical about their causes that things get out of hand. Examples of this extreme behavior are the

Oklahoma City bombing, the Heaven's Gate cult and some of the IRA or Taliban followers. Many of the people who attend the holistic or New Age festivals have this trait cluster.

Idealism could be directed toward hero worship, a ship to sail, a slum to clear or an environmental cause. Individuals with this trait are deeply hurt when one of their chosen "heroes" falls from the pedestal upon which they placed him or her. Idealistic people do not like to "make do," or "compromise," when their principles, their heroes or standards are involved. They tend to become very bitter when others fail them or if the situation is less than perfect. Honest mistakes, errors and imperfections are major catastrophes for which, in their eyes, there is no forgiveness.

Because Idealistic individuals are so dedicated to perfection, they are tireless workers who give their all "freely" to the field or cause of their choice. In personal relationships this trait can be very challenging; High Idealists end up being disappointed much of the time because they may harbor high expectations for their partners.

If you have this trait, learn to accept others on their own terms, remembering that no one is perfect. Expect nothing more of others than that which they give. Learn to acknowledge their achievements even though they may not come up to your expectations. When you hear yourself saying, "If it can't be perfect, I want none of it." Stop to think what you may be passing up.

Individuals who are more realistic (high set ears) are generally more practical and down to earth. Their standards are not as high as the Idealistic person. If you are more realistic, you might want to set higher standards and not just make do. Demand high standards from those working with you and don't let others get away with less than the best.

RELATIONSHIPS

Idealistic individuals will feel they have found the perfect mate with whom they will share the perfect life together. They put their partners and their relationships on pedestals and assume their significant others have the same standards and expectations as themselves. Then they wonder why the relationships come crashing down around them. Couples need to check in with each other to make sure they both have the same expectations.

CHILDREN

These are the dreamers; they sometimes live in a world of their own. They want the perfect world, the perfect family. They often have a make-believe friend.

CAREERS

This trait would be seen in people in ministers, psychologists, social workers, teachers, personal coaches, film directors or writers.

FAMOUS FACES · IDEALISTIC

Mahatma Gandhi, Richard Gere, and Pakistan President Pervez Musharraf.

ACQUISITIVE

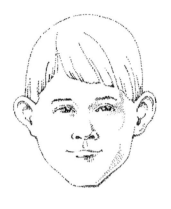 

EARS CUPPED OUT	EARS FLAT AGAINST THE HEAD
High acquisitive	Low acquisitive

The High Acquisitive trait can be identified by the combination of protruding ears and oval forehead. Individuals with this combination of features collect everything. Every nail, piece of paper, wood, empty boxes, piece of string – you name it. They are loath to toss things out – just in case it might be useful another day. There comes a time when the piles get too high and can take over the house.

The High Acquisitive trait also indicates an individual has the ability to hear sound well; they can hear conversations three tables away. When people with such ears have their ears clipped back, this will take away some of the natural ability to hear sound well. One woman said that her children thought her hearing was not as good after she had an operation to correct her protruding ears.

RELATIONSHIPS

When individuals have protruding ears, an oval forehead and close-set eyes, they tend to be very possessive. They become very jealous if the other person in their life dares to pay too much attention to someone else. If their partners should get admiring glances from other people or appear to be spending too much time with persons of the opposite sex at a party, individuals with this trait combination would perceive this as a threat to their relationship. Their philosophy is, my partner or friend is mine and mine alone, and is not to be shared with anyone.

If you have the tendency to become very possessive of your partner, loosen up or that other person in your life will feel stifled, and may well leave you.

CHILDREN

No one should throw out another person's things before asking the owner's permission. This includes parents. Always ask the child first if he wants to keep that item; don't just throw it out because you think it has no further use. One father would go through his son's toys and discard what he thought was not needed. The child was devastated although he dared not tell his father. He would retreat into his own world, feeling hurt that something so special to him was thrown out.

HOBBIES

Collect stamps; art if you have high Aesthetic Appreciation (straight eyebrows); antiques if you have Backward Balance (more head in back of ears); and old cars. If your forehead is flat, collect books. If you have rounded ears, collect music.

FAMOUS FACES · HIGH ACQUISITIVE

Prince Harry, Mikhail Gorbachev, William Hague of the English Conservative Party, and tennis player Tim Henman.

 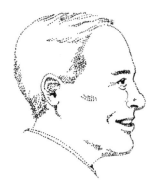

MORE HEAD
BEHIND THE EAR

Backward balance

MORE FACE
IN FRONT OF THE EAR

Forward balance

This is a time orientation trait, basing decisions on thoughts about past experiences, what is happening today, or in the future and is determined by looking at head proportions to determine whether there is more head in the front of the ear or behind the ear. If there is more head in front of the ear, this individual will think in terms of the present and the future and have Forward Balance.

The Forward Balance trait also measures how much a person needs recognition or appreciation. Everyone needs some degree of recognition; however, when that need is significant, that individual wants to be in the limelight. Forward Balance individuals love the applause from an audience and will sometimes "ham it up" in order to get that attention.

Individuals with this trait love to call attention to themselves, whether it is from loud behavior, getting praise for putting on a good show, or simply by drawing attention to themselves by making negative remarks about other people. They can be so full of themselves that consideration of other people's feelings does not come into their thoughts. In the extreme of this trait, these individuals may come across as being extremely inconsiderate. Lisa likes to get attention and will make noises or make people laugh, anything that will draw attention to her. When she teases a waiter or waitress, her husband gets really annoyed. He is embarrassed by his wife's behavior.

This Forward Balance trait is often seen in leaders of countries, groups or organizations. They are more dynamic, and set policies faster in the moment because they think in terms of the present and the future. They are lively companions and often the life and the soul of the party. Additionally, this trait is found in people who are performers, teachers, professional sports players or any profession that puts them "on stage."

If you are have the trait of Forward Balance, make sure you take the time to recognize what others have achieved. Don't bring attention to yourself at the cost of others.

People with Backward Balance have more of the head behind the ear. Backward Balance individuals compare tradition and past experiences to present situations. These are the individuals who tend to hang on to past memories – whether positive or negative. Sometimes they sound like a "broken record," going over and over about all the negative aspects of their life. What was done to them years ago is never to be forgiven. If we hear their woes once, we hear them a thousand times over. They will re-run past negative conversations over and over to the point that it almost obsessive. At times it is hard for them to turn off the inner chatter.

If you are a Backward Balance person and find yourself going over about something in your mind or verbally, catch yourself. Develop ways to let your thoughts go. Imagine a river running through your mind, washing away all of the negative thoughts. Or better still, deliberately find something more positive to think about.

Backward Balanced people enjoy recognition, but more for what they have achieved or accomplished. They are more comfortable in the background and seldom seek the limelight. They are more interested in what they are doing and how they will accomplish their goals of today. They tend to be very considerate and will bend over backwards to help you. They enjoy history or anything related to historical interests such as archeology and genealogy. Combined with the High Acquisitive trait (cupped-out ears), they will enjoy collecting old coins, antiques or anything of a historical nature.

When someone has Backward Balance, intense feelings (long thumb), and Low Tolerance (close-set eyes), this could indicate the person might be vindictive. They may have stored bad memories or anger for years; any incident or something someone says will suddenly trigger off their pent-up anger. If you have this trait, try to focus on what is working today. When family members have this trait there is a tendency for them to be very unforgiving of the past. It causes many rifts between parents and children and between siblings. Holding on to the bad memories serves no purpose, let them go. Fill your life with the good things that are happening today, and the pleasant memories of the past.

Individuals with this trait have a tendency to hide their light under a bushel. They need to learn how to blow their own horns and get the recognition deserved for the accomplishments achieved, no matter how small. In some cultures, such as the United States, where individuals share their accomplishments more freely, this is encouraged.

The challenge for individuals with Backward Balance is to let go of the grudges. Remember to look ahead not look back. Hanging on to negative associations can drain the energy, it serves no purpose in our lives other than the lesson learned.

CHILDREN

The Forward Balance child will need recognition. Parents need to make sure that this trait in their child is channeled into the right direction. Don't wait for your child to act out, to praise him; beat him to it and praise him liberally for what he has done. If such children don't get the recognition needed in the home, or they are not given tasks or activities that will challenge them, they may well end up joining gangs or similar peer groups. Get them involved with activities such as the theatre, sports, gymnastics, ballet or any activity where they get attention. Understanding children's traits from the very beginning will help to avoid the challenges that confront parents. In a television interview with youngsters who had committed various crimes, it was evident that many of them were High Self-confident (wide face), Competitive and Forward Balance.

The foundation of our youth begins with the understanding of their strengths, challenges and innate abilities. The Career and Personality Assessment Profile (CAPA Profile) will help parents, teachers and counselors to get an insight into how to work with these traits. Many adopted and foster children just don't "fit in" with their adopted family. Understanding their traits will give parents some vital clues on how best to work with them. It will help to guide the children in the direction that supports their innate abilities.

FAMOUS FACES · FORWARD BALANCE

Saddam Hussein, Pierce Brosnan, Madonna and Dame Judy Dench.

INDECISION

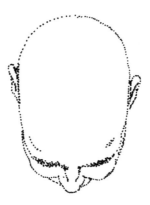

ONE EAR IS FURTHER BACK THAN THE OTHER
Indecision

The physical feature associated with the trait of Indecision can be observed when looking at the person in front of you face-on. Notice if one ear appears to be farther forward than the other. If this is really noticeable, individuals with this trait will go back and forth in making a decision. You think they have made up their minds and suddenly it's a different story. Dawn stated she found making decisions very difficult, so she would ask all of her friends, or anyone who she met, what should she do. Based on their advice, she would then make a decision. If an individual has a lot of asymmetry in the face (Mood Swings), this will create even more difficulty in decision-making. If the person's life is out of balance or stressed, he or she will become very unpredictable. If you have this trait, make a decision and stay with it unless there is good reason to change your mind.

If you find you really cannot make up your mind, go for a vigorous walk, work out at a gym or go for a bike ride. This will help to clear your head and you will be in a better state of mind for making a decision. So next time you're in a flux, try exercising. It works.

Chapter Twelve: The Head

CONFIDENCE

NARROW FACE
Build confidence

WIDE FACE
High self-confidence

Self-confidence is determined by the width of the face through the outer edge of the eyebrows compared with the height of the face from the chin to the turn of the forehead.

Self-confidence is a feeling, not an intellectual awareness of one's potential. In other words, innate self-confidence is the individual's basic feeling about himself or herself. Individuals who have wide faces feel confident and assured in the face of challenges or environmental circumstances. They assume they can take on anything whether or not they have the knowledge or experience. They think they are smart enough to handle any situation and then wonder later why they fail. The only time they feel challenged is when they take on extremely large responsibilities or challenges. They are very self-sufficient and rely on themselves to handle most situations. However, this is a feeling – not necessarily a fact. As one person shared with me, "I fake it 'til I make it." It never occurred to her that she may not have enough experience or information to take on a new project. She was comfortable learning on the job.

High Self-confidence is a trait that is often seen in many leaders such as Winston Churchill, Edward Kennedy, Saddam Hussein and Boris Yeltsin. These are the people who enjoy a leading role in life. It would be hard for them to stay in the background and play a supportive role. On the other hand, individuals with narrow faces gain their confidence through knowledge; they tend to over-learn before taking on anything new. They take class after class until they feel confident that they have enough information to start their new business or career.

A bright engineer (narrow face), who was well known for his expertise in his field, was asked to give a presentation to some prominent engineers in Germany. This was the first time he had given a presentation to such a distinguished group. When the time came to give his paper, he was terrified and fumbled through the presentation. The tension inside him was agonizing. If his employers had prepared him beforehand, his presentation would probably have been very successful. Instead, he left the presentation feeling he had not come up to the group's expectations. The whole experience devastated him. If his manager had said to him, "Mark, this is new for you. Here is someone you can work with to help you prepare the talk," this approach would have taken much of the fear out of the presentation.

One of the major complaints by employees is that there is not enough training for people who are facing new situations or positions in the company. This is particularly true for narrow-faced people who feel the need to know more to feel comfortable than do the highly confident people. Many employees with narrow faces have walked out because the thought of facing new situations with no support in place was too daunting. If managers just took the time to put in place a training program, it would save the company far more than the cost of the training.

Low self-esteem is often seen in people with narrow faces. If they are brought up in non-supportive environments, it will take quite some time before they can believe in themselves. One woman was extremely fearful of stepping out from her secure life. She did not need to work; yet she had the desire to find her own niche in life, but fear was holding her back. With some coaching she was able to move her life forward and work through the fear.

Individuals with narrow faces are willing to stand back and learn from others and evaluate situations. They are more aware of their own limitations. Once they are knowledgeable in their field, they have all the confidence in the world. Until they have the knowledge needed, they are unlikely to confront the world. Other traits such as forcefulness, competitiveness and progressiveness will make them appear more confident than they actually feel inside. These traits tend to push them out on the edge. They wonder why they keep putting themselves in such challenging situations. To others, people with low self-confidence persons will appear to hesitate before taking on anything new. They presume their inadequacy most of the time.

Highly self-confident people look as though they are in charge. You can spot them as soon as you enter a room because they radiate self-assurance. Even though they may not be talking to you, you can feel they are important and people to be reckoned with. When they speak, their voices are stronger and more powerful. They take command of the situation. When confronted or challenged by others, they will raise the volume of their voice in order to be in control.

The powerful presence displayed by highly self-confident people can be just as much a problem as a benefit. They may use their power to play out their own fantasies at the expense of others. This is often seen in countries where there is so much conflict going on. They become bullies and are more interested in protecting and building their own image than supporting others. Saddam Hussein and Slobodan Milosevic are prime examples of the trait running out of control.

The highly self-confident person needs to learn that problems come along with the powers. Just because he feels self-assured doesn't make him right in what he wants. If you have this trait, learn to be a leader who works with and for people. Be an inspiration to your followers.

Where the highly self-confident person is self-assured, tasks or situations beyond their realm of expertise will overwhelm the narrow-faced person. People with low self-confidence are intensely aware of their limitations and, consequently, are more apt to stay with what is familiar or comfortable rather than strike out boldly in new fields. Again, this depends on other traits that may support or diminish self-confidence. In order to rise above discouragement, they need to have some real incentive, a real goal. Their risk is to surrendering to self-doubt and old fear-oriented reactions, especially when confronted with meeting new people or in new situations or challenges. If you have this trait, think about the times when you have pulled through, despite the uncertainty. Keep in mind that fear is only lack of information and experience. You can achieve both.

The person who has the higher self-confidence is the one with the final authority. They can be very impatient when they see a hesitancy or weakness in the other people. They may "take the project right out of their hand" just to make the point, "See I can do it, what's wrong with you?"

This can be a vicious cycle. The first time narrow-faced individuals are confronted with new assignments they doubt their own ability to handle them successfully and so hesitate to begin. The confident person can see no reason why they don't jump right in and do it. After a while, because the wide-faced person constantly jumps in and takes over, resentment sets in.

If the two people in a relationship have a similar width of face, chances are there will be better compatibility. If the differences are significant, what each partner at first liked in the other will become an irritation. The wide-faced individual will come across as being more dominant, and in some cases crush their partner's confidence. They'll want to call the shots. Advice to highly self-confident partners: Be supportive and keep silent about what you think ought to be done, until asked. When needed, offer constructive advice or suggestions on another way that something can be done.

JUDY, WHO HAS A NARROW FACE, WAS ELECTED PRESIDENT OF A WOMEN'S GROUP. SHE HAD NEVER BEEN IN THAT ROLE BEFORE AND FOR THE FIRST SIX MONTHS SHE WAS TERRIFIED. MANY A TIME SHE WANTED TO "NOT TURN UP" BECAUSE THE POSITION WAS CAUSING HER SO MUCH ANXIETY. ONCE SHE KNEW THE ROPES, SHE DID AN EXCELLENT JOB. HAD THERE BEEN SOMEONE TO ASSIST HER THOSE FIRST FEW MONTHS, IT WOULD HAVE BEEN AN EASIER TRANSITION.

The low self-confident person in a relationship with a highly self-confident individual may feel their partner has no faith in them. Low self-confident individuals feel all their decisions are being made for them and are they are forced into doing things they would rather not do. Narrow-faced persons will feel there is no appreciation for what they do and no respect for them as a person. When the wide-faced person laughs at the little things that please or upset their narrow-faced partners, the narrow faced person will feel their partner is trying to put them down and then feel bad. This makes it harder for them to speak up in fear of being made fun of.

If you are more self-confident, support the growth and creativity of those who are less confident. When you are working with someone with a narrow face, recognize that person needs to be familiar with new situations first. Be prepared to support them in situations that are new to them.

On the positive aspects of low self-confidence individuals are aware of their limitations and are quick to seek out others or take classes to enhance their knowledge.

However, individuals with this trait tend to undersell themselves. Rather than fight pressure, they may conform or run away from it. They may feel inadequate because they lack either experience or knowledge needed to take on a new task. Once they have the knowledge, the situation will seem less daunting. They'll have all the confidence in the world.

CHILDREN

When working with children who are highly confident, the parent needs to be more assertive, especially if the parent has low self-confidence. Otherwise, when the child becomes a teenager, the problems of control and discipline will be difficult to cope with. The parents need to be consistent in how they raise their child and be supportive of each other.

The wide-faced child must be willing to take directions and do so cheerfully from the person in authority. She needs to learn to accept supervision gracefully and to learn to be good follower, so she can later be a good leader. The parents must demand unquestioned obedience. Parents should give the child larger responsibilities and opportunities whenever possible, and give her toys, books or games that are designed for children two years older than her. Parents should read her stories about exciting happenings in real life.

Narrow-faced children need to be exposed to all kinds of experiences under supervision, with each experience to be taken in small doses, just one step at a time. Once the basic knowledge of what to expect is there, they are able to handle the new situation easily. Parents need to support and acknowledge their children's achievements whether small or large. If children with narrow faces are also sequential thinkers parents shouldn't hurry them or try to skip levels. It's best to let the children grow and learn at their own pace. Parents should give them new assignments one at a time and make sure the children understand each step of the way.

FAMOUS FACES · BUILDS SELF-CONFIDENCE
Elizabeth Hurley, John Lennon, and Abraham Lincoln.

FAMOUS FACES · HIGH SELF-CONFIDENCE
Colin Powell, Pakistan President Pervez Musharraf, William Hague, Margaret Thatcher, and Hillary Clinton.

TO CONSERVE, TO CONSTRUCT

OVAL FOREHEAD

The maintainer

SQUARE FOREHEAD

Likes to start new things

The tendency to either preserve and save what one has as opposed to engaging new projects and letting go of old things can be determined by the shape of the forehead from the outside edge of the eyebrow to the forehead following the hairline. Does the head look oval or square? In order to determine the exact shape, place the ball (region of the palm directly under the index finger) of each hand on the outside points of the eyebrows left and right. With your fingers pointing vertically, let them gradually come to a rest on the outer edge of the curvature of the forehead. Does the immediate area at the top of the index finger feel rounded or does it feel square? If rounded this will indicate the person has the trait we call Conservation. If square, this individual will make many career changes throughout his or her life (Construction). To better understand where to look for the curve, look at the line just under the hairline on the sketch.

High Conservation individuals like to preserve what they already have. They will hold on to things just in case they will be useful another day. If this trait is also combined with High

Acquisitiveness (protruding ears), these people can be "pack rats" or hoarders. Unlike individuals with square foreheads (Construction), they have a hard time throwing things out. They will hold on to their possessions for years, including screws, small pieces of wood, paper with outdated information and old magazines. To others, this is just "junk" that is collecting dust that often gets thrown out by a roommate or spouse, who perceives the items as having no further value. If you are guilty of throwing other people's things out, perhaps you should first go through the things together to see what the other person would like to keep.

For the High Conservation individual, home and family are very important. Their comfort zone is the center of their lives and their home base means everything to them. They love to fix up old things, remodel the home, and rearrange the furniture.

Individuals with this trait like to nurture. When this trait is combined with Growing Trend (large ear lobes) the person will likely enjoy gardening. This trait is often seen in the hotel industry, hospitals; healthcare; dietitians, chemists, psychologists and project managers; or any career that is focused on maintaining or preserving. These individuals are great at maintaining friends and client relationships. This is also a good trait to have in sales or customer service.

High Conservation individuals are the people who love to work out at gyms or participate in any other activities that are done on a regular basis. High Construction people with square foreheads will go to the gym a couple of times then drop out. They don't like doing things on a regular basis unless they are really passionate about the activity or it is needed to improve their skills. They don't like repetition. They like new things! They want to start things from scratch rather than remodel. They are less likely to hang on to things that could be useful another day. They don't like to have clutter around them – their philosophy is if they need something, they can always go out and purchase the item again. High Construction individuals have a tendency to throw things out and start afresh, a trait that appears wasteful to Conservation people.

Once the High Construction person has done something, it's finished. "Been there, done that." It would be extremely boring to them to maintain a project for a long period of time – the same with client relationships. They will see the client few times and then want them to be on their merry way. They lose interest in anything that repeats itself too often. Going on the same walk, doing the same thing day after day – anything that has routine, they will find boring. They will make many career changes throughout their lives.

High Construction people tune in to whatever's new like ducks take to water: new ideas, new projects, new materials to work with or moving to new locations. When they focus on new projects, they put all their energy and time to developing it or getting it off the ground. All else fades into the background; they will resent being pulled away from their project to attend to less interesting activities.

The negative aspects of this trait: they may be extravagant by not holding onto something in case it could be useful, or making do with what they have. They are inclined to spare no expense to have what's new when the "old" would actually serve just as well.

Individuals with this trait tend to be overly absorbed in their careers, often to the point where they neglect themselves and their families. This was a problem for a young couple. The husband was constantly at work, spending very little time with his wife. For him to take time out was an interruption. After a consultation, the husband agreed to set aside some time each week for them to have quality time together.

Women who have this trait will find staying at home very boring, they need to fill their day with a part-time job or do volunteer work. If there is a mixture of both Conservation (oval forehead) and Construction (square forehead) part of the individual will want to be at home, while the other part would like to be working. An ideal situation for these individuals would be to work out of the home.

The idea of retirement does not appeal to people who have the Construction trait. The mere thought of it is scary. What will they do with all of that time? They need to have a purpose in life or they get bored very quickly.

If you have a square forehead, learn to "make-do" with what is already available rather than rushing out and getting something new. When you find yourself saying, "Let's start from scratch," you should stop and check to see what is on hand.

Because they let their careers dominate their lives, High Construction types need to pay attention to the "creature comforts" – meeting their own basic needs and the needs of their families – and to their own health. They need to schedule time for family and close friends. They need to learn that life does not have to be all about work, and schedule some time to play.

CAREERS

Counseling, health related-fields, teaching, electronic engineering, and botany.

FAMOUS FACES · HIGH CONSERVATION

John Cleese, John McEnroe, Andrew Lloyd Weber, and Madonna.

THINKING STYLE

FOREHEAD SLOPES BACKWARD   FOREHEAD IS VERTICAL

Objective thinker   Sequential thinker

Looking at the side profile of the head, does the angle of the
forehead slope backward or is it more vertical? If it slopes backward,
this individual is quick to think and respond in the moment. These
are your Objective Thinkers. Those with the vertical foreheads prefer
a step-by-step approach and we call them Sequential Thinkers.

The various "thinking" traits have to do with how people think,
not what they think about, or how much quality there is to their
thinking. "How" breaks down into two categories. Objective
Thinkers are inclined to allow their automatic reactions determine
their thoughts in the moment, based on past experiences. Sequential
Thinkers are inclined to consciously process "new" ideas or challenges through a rational and logical thought process. In other
words, Objective Thinkers deal in reactions to something and
Subjective Thinkers deal with the "thing or situation" itself.

The Objective Thinkers (sloped forehead) are the quick deci-
sion-makers and often jump to conclusions or "second guess" what
other people are going to say or do. They instantly respond to what
is going on around them and are often irritated by people who

appear to be slower than themselves. They quickly see the broad picture without necessarily needing all of the details. This trait can often be seen in individuals who excel at sports, activities such as snowboarding, downhill skiing, football and tennis. This trait is a plus for any activity for which quick reaction is a benefit. The challenge for objective thinkers is that they tend to jump to conclusions before getting all of the information.

Clyde, a newspaper reporter, who has the Objective Thinking trait, interviewed me about my book. He took about five minutes to get a general overview of face reading, and presumed he knew all there was to know. The article was a poor representation of my work, leaving me very disappointed. Three years later I produced another book. Despite my efforts to find someone else in the newspaper office to write an article on face reading, Clyde decided it was his job to do the interview. My heart sank.

His opening comment was, "Tell me something about myself." I told him he jumped to conclusions. He said: "You mean I don't get all the details?" I proceeded to give him a personal reading. He wrote the best article I've seen in years. Many friends called me and asked how I did it. If you have this trait, when necessary, take more time to check all the details. This could save you both time and money.

The Objective Thinking trait is a plus where quick decision-making is part of the job for example, paramedics, firefighters and people who race cars will find their response to situations in the moment will be much faster.

When an Objective Thinker is in a relationship with a Sequential Thinker, these opposite traits will cause some annoyances. The Objective Thinker will see the Sequential Thinker as being deliberately slow. He or she will try to hurry their partner up which then creates more pressure, which could turn into a heated argument. If you have either trait, don't expect everyone to move at your speed.

On the other hand, Sequential Thinkers are turned off by fast, "high pressure" sales or tactics. They need time to examine each step of the process. If they miss part of the information due to rapid delivery, they will get lost and the subsequent information will go over their heads. Once they understand the missing piece, it becomes very clear. Under pressure, their minds may go blank, particularly during exams or if a test is suddenly presented to them – they know the answers but their minds freeze. Whether it is a last-minute test, or a response to an emergency situation, they need the time to think through their decisions. It is very difficult for them to "speed up."

This Sequential Thinking trait is often a challenge for children in school because they appear to be slow learners and are misunderstood. Many children with this trait are labeled as slow learners or are accused of not concentrating because they didn't hear what was being said. This was the case for Steve, a 12-year-old boy. His teacher thought he had a learning disability and recommended that he go into a special class for slow learners. In order for Steve to stay in the class, the school requested his parents come in and meet with the school psychologist. The first words to the parents from the counselor were, "What is he doing in this class? He is reading at college level." Steve's style of learning was misunderstood by his teacher. If she had recognized his preferred learning style, she would not have recommended the special class. There must be hundreds of children who have experienced this frustration. Hopefully teachers or parents reading this section will be able to better understand and work with children who have this trait.

When interacting with Sequential Thinkers, check to make sure they have understood what information you have covered before going on to the next step. Give them time to assimilate the new information. When appropriate, hand them a written outline so that they can follow or review the information ahead of time. When possible, give a general review at the end.

If the Sequential Thinking person asks you for help in performing some task, make sure you explain the basic steps that lead up to the solution or she'll be completely lost by any additional instruction. She will shut down in frustration and won't hear what is being said if she hasn't understood a previous point. Give her all the steps needed before moving on too quickly. This has nothing to do with intellect; it is related to how she processes the information. When your are giving Sequential Thinkers instructions on the computer make sure they understand the first steps; otherwise if you do not establish that they know how to get to "B" without first explaining, "A" they will be completely lost.

Sequential Thinkers like to get to their destinations and appointments in plenty of time. If it is left to the last minute, they feel rushed and experience a

KEEP IN MIND THAT SEQUENTIAL THINKERS LIKE TO UNDERSTAND EACH STEP OF THE INFORMATION. THEY DO NOT LIKE TO BE RUSHED INTO DECISION-MAKING. ONCE THEY MAKE THEIR DECISION, IT REFLECTS THEIR FULL UNDERSTANDING OF THE PRODUCT OR CONCEPT. THE CHALLENGE FOR THEM IS TO RESPOND TO A SITUATION QUICKLY WHEN NEEDED, BOTH IN THOUGHT AND ACTION.

high sense of anxiety that they will not arrive on time. They need to let their travelling companions know they would like to leave by a specific time. Just explain that it is more comfortable that way – it takes off the pressure.

To the Objective Thinker, Sequential Thinkers appear to be very slow. Sometimes when the Sequential Thinker is asked a question, they will mull things over before responding. This can be very annoying to the person with the opposite trait, who will attempt to hurry them up by saying, "What's taking you so long to respond?"

Another tendency the Sequential Thinker has is to start a conversation in the middle of a thought; the other person won't have a clue what they're talking about. This was a challenge that a school principal experienced when he first took up his new position. He said people used to look at him with blank stares, not understanding what on earth he was talking about. He quickly learned to start at the beginning.

CHILDREN

If your child or student has this trait, make sure their questions are answered or that they have fully understood the instructions. If you change your plans for the day, give them plenty of warning. If it is a last minute change, discuss with them the reasons why first, this will help them to change gears. As parents, you need to let the teacher know that your child has this trait. This will avoid some of the frustration that children experience at school. These observations are not known to most school teacher's.

CAREERS

Firefighter, police work, stand-up comedian, sales, paramedic, newscaster, taxi driver or any career where quick reaction is needed.

FAMOUS FACES · OBJECTIVE THINKERS

Andre Agassi, Rudolph Giuliani, Venus and Serena Williams.

FAMOUS FACES · SEQUENTIAL THINKERS

Tom Hanks.

IMAGINATION

MOUNDS JUST BELOW THE HAIRLINE
Imagination

Imagination is indicated by the raised mounds that are formed on the left and right side of the forehead, roughly an inch below the hairline. The more pronounced they are, the greater the person's imagination.

"Imagination" is a word that conveys the power to visualize freely without getting too far-fetched into fantasies. Imagination allows a person to be specific in their visualizations. An individual with High Imagination is able to form mental images or concepts easily.

High Imagination individuals tend to be very creative and inventive. They can be lots of fun to be around. For them, the enjoyment is participating in an "adventure" such as planning a trip or designing a new game. If they have Design Appreciation (Inverted V eyebrows) and High Organization (half-moon eyebrows) traits this will add to their creativeness.

High Imagination can also create strong negative images. Julie, the mother of a young infant, panicked when she wondered what would happen to her baby if she were to faint or pass out. All she could imagine was that her baby would crawl to the toilet, fall in, and drown. This mental image was so strong for her that she signed up for a first aid class to cope with emergencies. Sometimes her imagination would take her to extremes – similar to creating a horror movie in her mind. She would be so caught up in the imaginary situation that it almost seemed real to her.

If you have this trait try not to let your imagination get carried away into negative images; immediately turn your thoughts to more positive situations.

CAREERS

If the forehead is very round and curves out like the sphere of a football this trait indicates that he/she has a natural gift for coming up with original ideas. I often see this trait in cartoonists and with critical perception, television cameramen. This trait can be seen in both men and women who are extremely artistic, although it may not manifest as an artistic talent. Instead it could be fashion design, web design, make up artist or any career that has a creative outlet.

FAMOUS FACES · IMAGINATION

Tom Hanks, Halle Berry, and author John Grisham.

HIGH IMPATIENCE / HIGH CONCENTRATION

FOREHEAD SLOPES IN OUTSIDE THE EYEBROWS	FOREHEAD SLOPES OUTWARD OUTSIDE THE EYEBROWS
Impatience	High concentration

These two traits can be determined from the same area on the head. If the forehead has an inward slope just outside the outer edge of the eyebrow, like one side of an "A-frame tent," this indicates impatience. If the forehead slopes outward, this person will possess an ability to concentrate. Concentration is the ability to keep one's mind on a line of thought and follow it through. Conversely, Impatience indicates the individual with this trait desires to quickly finish what he is doing and move on to the next project.

This is different from Tolerance. Tolerance is to put up with something on a long-term basis; Impatience is an irritation that happens in the moment. Typically, when Impatient individuals have to wait in line, or people do something to irritate them, there is an instant feeling of aggravation throughout their entire being. Individuals with High Concentration have a long attention span, whether thinking, observing or doing. A young child with this trait can amaze adults by how long and intently they will engage in an activity that absorbs them.

An individual with high concentration can take a line of thought and carry through the thinking necessary for an entire project. When this trait is combined with High Analytical (eyelids hidden) plus Low Tolerance (close-set eyes), the resulting individuals are born researchers. They are mentally patient and capable of carrying out jobs that may be laborious, or spending hours trying to fix a problem. At times, High Concentration individuals start thinking about something they have seen or read, and may appear to be a "thousand miles away." Often when they sit down to read a book or newspaper, they become so absorbed that they may be oblivious to everyone and everything around them.

A High Concentration husband who was absorbed in his hobby failed to smell the dinner burning. His wife, on returning in her car, noted smoke pouring out of the window and immediately rushed in to find the charcoal remains of the meal. The husband hadn't even noticed!

In social situations, people with this trait need to make sure they are paying attention to what is going on around them. If this trait is also combined with close-set eyes, these individuals can get buried in their own thoughts or any activity they are engaging in. If you want to interrupt them, just quietly say, "I need you in a moment," or just lay a hand on their shoulder to get their attention.

The person who is less impatient has a mind inclined to move rapidly from one thing to another. They welcome interruptions (if they have High Tolerance/wide-set eyes) just to take a break from what they are doing. If you are studying and you're struggling to stay focused, try giving yourself a break every few hours. This will give you the time needed to break away from what you're doing without the nagging thought, "You have to stay at what you're doing." This helps to balance the day and you'll get far more accomplished. You will approach the project with a fresh mind and determination.

High Impatient people are more impatient with others than they are with themselves. They know the reason why they haven't finished certain things. But they will sit impatiently in the car waiting for the other passenger to put in an appearance. All they can think about is the next thing they want to do. Any delay will be very irritating to them.

High Impatient individuals are valuable in situations where time is at a premium. For example, an airport employee moving baggage quickly to get it on the plane, or a personal secretary swiftly getting messages through. The disadvantage is that Impatient individuals may make others unhappy by keeping after them to speed up. They take things out of the other person's hands in order to speed up the action.

Highly impatient people, who also have the trait of low tolerance, get irritated at things not happening fast enough to suit them, such as an irritated car driver having to wait in rush hour traffic – typical behavior of New York taxi drivers or those of any other big city.

If you are impatient and you're finding yourself getting irritated, take time out to have a break. Realize it can be very irritating to the other person when you appear to be snatching things away from them, or trying to jump the line. Walk around the block or go and do something different – it will help to refresh you.

HIGH COMPETITIVE / LOW COMPETITIVE

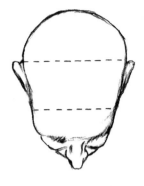 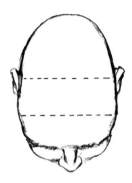

HEAD IS WIDER AT BACK
COMPARED TO THE FRONT

High competitive

HEAD IS NARROWER ABOVE
THE EARS COMPARED
WITH THE FRONT

Low competitive

The shape of the head indicates if an individual likes to meet situations head on or whether he tends to hesitate or be more "roundabout" in addressing things. The head shape also indicates if a person is more competitive, or tends to dream about their ideas rather than take action.

If the head is wider above the ear compared to the front, this will indicate the person will be naturally competitive. Ross Perot and many politicians and CEOs of companies will have this competitive trait. It is their competitiveness that drives them to beat their competition and succeed.

If we were to look down from above at the head of a competitive person, it would appear to be a wedge shape. Individuals with this wedge-shaped head love to compete. They get an enormous thrill from the enjoyment of winning. For them, competition is what it is all about and nothing beats winning. Individuals who are low competitive will have a head that is wider in the front than

YOU CAN READ A FACE LIKE A BOOK

above the ears. They are turned off by the competitive nature of others and scorn such people who are so competitive.

One can assess one's competitive nature by looking at the side of the head, immediately in line with the center of the ear. If the head is wider at that point in comparison to the halfway mark between the ear and front of the forehead, the more competitive the person will be (High Competitive). When the head is wider in the front, this indicates the individual is less competitive. Think of the head as a slice of pie or a wedge shape. If the head is wider above the ear: Competitive. If the head is wider in the front: Low Competitive.

Highly competitive people are the high achievers. They constantly strive to outdo the other person or compete within themselves to achieve better results. Because of this trait, they accomplish and produce more results. We see this trait in professional athletes, salespeople, politicians, CEOs or any leadership or management position. The wider the head is above the ear the more competitive individuals are in all aspects of their life.

Competitive individuals have the desire to win. In the extreme, these individuals often come across as being very aggressive – and may appear hostile to others. There is a great sense of wanting to get ahead at all costs. When High Competitive individuals feel challenged, they will tend to fight back. They want to win. They need to concentrate on the pleasure of doing well rather than focusing on winning regardless of the odds or how they win.

Pat is very competitive and likes to exceed her daily goals and complete them early. She puts a time on each goal and then competes against the clock. She also likes to compete with her husband's attention. He has a natural rapport with people and she wants people to like her as much as they do her husband. Others see her as being pushy. She could not understand why they saw her that way. She didn't see her behavior that way. It is natural for her to push ahead; this petite person is quite a powerhouse. She finds one way to balance this energy is to exercise; she feels so much better for it and the rest of the day goes better. Bill, another competitive client of mine, does not like to compete unless he knows he can win. He wants to be the best and wants the world to know it.

Another client shared with me that when people are blocking her way, she almost feels emotionally violent and very intolerant. When she wants to do something, nothing will hold her back. Sometimes these very traits are what people hate her for.

The energy of the High Competitive person can scare people off. When companies are looking for a "race horse" (slang for a competitive executive) and get one, they're not quite sure how to handle their energy. At work, when things need to he done, the High Competitive will jump several levels of management in order to get the projects accomplished – finding it very aggravating when people do not move on things.

If you have this trait learn not to be so aggressive when it is not appropriate. Know when to turn it off. This is a great trait to have in sales.

Low Competitive individuals have no interest in competing. They play a sport for the pleasure and enjoyment. Winning is not important. To them, competitiveness takes the pleasure out of the activity. They like everyone to have a chance at winning.

I met Ann at an event in England. She expressed to me that she absolutely hated competition. She had been seeing a therapist for a number of months to help her get over the intense dislike of being around people who were so competitive. Both her sister and her mother were extremely competitive people, so this was a huge issue for Ann. After spending less than a minute with her, I explained to her that by nature she was not a competitive person and did not need to be. She looked at me in total astonishment that I was able to determine this in less than a minute. I asked her to describe what being competitive was for her.

You Can Read a Face Like a Book

Ann expressed her anger and resentment of how this had affected her life. I then asked her to move to another area of the room and describe to me what it would be like to be non-competitive. The tension left her face she looked very relaxed. What she described was who she was by nature. This took a load off her shoulders; she no longer needed to act in a way that was foreign and uncomfortable for her. Her goal was to become a professional singer, but the competitive nature of the business turned her off. I suggested she let her agent do the competing, leaving her to perfect her singing skills. She had such a look of relief as she departed.

A Low Competitive woman shared with me that she and her friends stayed at a cabin at Lake Tahoe for the weekend. In the evening, everyone except herself decided to play bridge. Beth did not like the aggressiveness of the game. All evening long she could hear them arguing and trying to outdo each other. She found the aggressive atmosphere most unpleasant; it put a damper on the weekend. The individuals involved in the game thought it was great fun. Winning was what it was all about for them – it gave them a high.

Individuals with this trait are not salespeople; they can do sales but they won't enjoy the constant pressure. Often times, in multi-level marketing, people fall in love with the product they represent. When it comes to selling, they hate it. There should be a way of screening people who are non-competitive; point out to them that this is the nature of multi-level marketing.

The High Competitive trait can be challenging in a relationship. If one individual is competitive and forceful and the other completely opposite, this can cause an emotional conflict. The High Competitive individual will wonder why his or her significant other just talks and talks about doing something and never gets around to doing it. The competitive person places his/her expectations on others. When these expectations are not realized, there will be constant frustration and possibly nagging. I met with a young man who said his mother was very competitive and forceful. She was constantly nagging her husband for not meeting her goals. Because her expectations were not met, this became a huge conflict in the family – a conflict that finally ended in divorce. Had she understood her own traits and those of her husband, much of the unpleasantness could have been avoided.

We need to accept who the other person is in a relationship, and to realize that our goals and aspirations may not be the same as our partners'. Some couples believe the myth, "things will change once we're married." Accept each other for who you are and work on mastering your own traits rather than pointing the finger at the other person.

CHILDREN

Children who are High Competitive need to have an outlet for that energy. Enroll them in a sport or activity that allows them to compete. Teach them to recognize and acknowledge other children's efforts even when they don't win. Show them how they can obtain their goals and aspirations without abusing others or appearing hostile.

CAREERS AND HOBBIES

Sales, police work, pilots, race car drivers, and all sports or any activity where the competitive energy can be channeled.

FAMOUS FACES · HIGH COMPETITIVE

William Hague, Vladimir Putin, Condoleeza Rice.

PROGRESSIVE

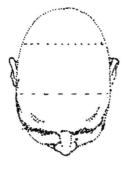 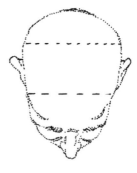

LOW PROGRESSIVE
Thinks more than acts

HIGH PROGRESSIVE
More aggressive

High Progressive means to "move on" things. Whether or not someone is progressive can be determined by comparing the width at the back of the head to the width at the front. Please refer to the sketch to get a better understanding of where this trait is located. The wider the head is at the back the more progressive the person.

If we were to view the head from above, it would appear to be pie-shaped. If the head is wider at the back than it is at the front, this indicates a High Progressive individual. If the frontal lobes are wider than the back, this indicates a tendency to procrastinate, put things off and generally reflect on life and ideas rather than acting on them. These are the Low Progressive people who talk about doing things but rarely put their ideas into action.

When a person's head is wider at the back compared to the front of the head, this indicates the individual is Progressive – built to act rather than think. Such people have long-range vision, and once they decide to do something, they will quickly move into action. Because of this, they are more likely to create their opportunities once they know which direction or actions to take. They are concerned with what they can do, not with what may stand in their way. However, others may perceive the High Progressive as only being interested in working toward his/her own goals and possibly feel they are being used to obtain those goals. Progressive individuals appear to be very aggressive and attack problems with full force, which may blind them to the consideration of other approaches that may be just as effective. They often have poor communication with their fellow workers because of their aggressive style.

Since this is the usual way they approach life, Progressive people usually achieve what they set out to do and are very positive in their approaches to new problems or situations. However, other people may feel shut out by their seemingly inconsiderate "shoving" at them. Often, the opportunities they make are for themselves and they make them at the expense of others – others' feelings and friendships. If this energy is not consciously directed, they walk over people in order to get ahead. Their attitude will be, "I will be the first up the steps and in the door; I will be the first in line." They may sacrifice others to get what they want and can be seen by others as cold, selfish and thoughtless.

ONE OF THE BENEFITS OF HIGH PROGRESSIVE INDIVIDUALS IS THAT THEY COME UP WITH AN IDEA, MAKE A PLAN AND TAKE THE NECESSARY STEPS FOR THE PROJECT TO BECOME A REALITY. THESE ARE THE PEOPLE WHO FORWARD THE ACTION.

There will be times when these individuals come across as being too aggressive and this may turn most people off. If this trait is combined with a more forceful nature and Competitive (the head is wider above the ears than in front), this could be a very aggressive person who will do what it takes to get to the top, even if it means loosing a few friends. If you have this trait, then use it when needed.

Otherwise, back off. Consider the price you are paying and ask yourself if it is worth it.

Low Progressive people are the dreamers. They seldom follow through on their ideas or commitments. They spend too much time thinking about what they are going to do rather than "doing it." They may start something then give it up half way through. Over a period of time, they are likely to stop "starting" and give up too quickly when confronted with pressure. This trait may deactivate their potential. Many people are puzzled by this behavior because the person with the Low Progressive is seen to have so much potential that others wonder why they don't move on with their lives. Low Progressives talk about their dreams but unless they schedule them in to their daily calendars they will remain only dreams.

Oftentimes Low Progressives will share their ideas with their friends. John's friends wait for him to take his idea to reality. Months and years go by and nothing happens. His friends presume he is no longer interested so they decide to develop it themselves. Or it could be that he's waited so long that someone else he has never met has launched the project.

David, who is less progressive, was a brilliant young man who was working for a large organization. His manager recognized the value that he was bringing to the company and offered him a more responsible position which, to the manager's surprise, David turned down. The manager could not understand why David was happy just doing what he was doing. The manager felt if he had half David's brains he would have been seeking a more responsible position in the company. I explained to his manager that David was really quite content in his current job. In fact, he would not find a more responsible position particularly satisfying because it brought with it responsibilities he did not want to take on.

The Low Progressive trait is often confused with laziness. I met a young man who had great ambitions but none of his goals had come to fruition. One of his frustrations was that he and his girl-friend were living with his family. His family constantly reminded him he would never amount to much. He was constantly told he was too lazy, that he had no talent or brains. It is devastating for anyone to be constantly told, "This is your life and don't expect much else." It is enough to crush anyone's spirits. I asked him if he believed what his family had been telling him. His response was no. I then asked him what could he do now that would start to make a change in his life. His fast response was, "Move out and find a place of my own." My next question was, "By when?" and he gave me a date with great conviction. The next day when I saw him he already had plans in place.

Individuals with the Low Progressive trait have dreams and aspirations. However, it takes a lot of energy to move on their ideas. Some describe the trait as feeling like they have a chain around their ankles. They desperately want to take their dreams to reality but it feels like some unseen force holds them back. They go to motivational seminars and leave ready to change their lives. After a couple of days, they start drifting back to old habits because their behavioral tendencies were never addressed. Things start to change only once they understand how to work with the trait.

If you have this trait and need to get something accomplished, create deadlines and commit to them. Don't let it be just another list that never gets looked at. Keep your lists short. Write down two to three things to do per day and only take on more when those tasks are completed. Short-term goals work better than long-term goals. If you have a vision or goal for the future, break it down into small bites; don't take on more than you can handle. In fact, if you have this trait stop here right now. Put a marker on this page so you can come back to it. Write out your vision or goals for the day, month and next six months and then give yourself a short list of things you need to do to accomplish them and by when. Put a date and time on them in your daily planner. When you look at your goals, how much do they inspire you?

I have in my office a parking meter that displays increments of twenty-five from zero to one hundred. I place the indicator on the marker that represents my level of excitement that I feel about my goal or task for the day. If the marker is at 50 percent that tells me I need to raise the level of energy around that task. Then I move the marker to 75 percent or even 100 percent. Then I look at what needs to be done now to raise the level of energy to complete the task. This idea was shared by Michael Losier, the owner of Teleclass International. He teaches a class called the Law of Attraction (that class is well worth the investment).

Individuals who are Low Progressive need to demand more of themselves if they want their dreams to become reality. If they have been asked to do something and they agree to do it, then they must stay to the commitment. In relationships, if your significant other asks you to do something, and you have this trait, make a plan and put it into your schedule. This will help to avoid the nagging about something not being done. Be more accountable for what you said you would do.

RELATIONSHIPS

If both people in the relationship are High Progressives, they need to pool their goals and ideas so that they are going in the same direction together. This will give them twice as much power.

If one person is Low Progressive, this can be a constant source of depression within the relationship. They may act as a "wet blanket" to the other person's energy. One of them wants to move on and take action while the other person may decide to "hang back" or "put off" making a decision. In this case, a compromise needs to be worked out that would allow the more aggressive person to achieve his or her goals, while at the same time not neglecting the other person who might not have that same motivation. This was the situation with a couple I knew who came to me for coaching. The wife desperately wanted to move; 12 years later, they were still in the same house. She had tried in every way to motivate her husband, with no results. He was the dreamer, and she was the competitive and progressive one. The situation was becoming a problem in their marriage; it was at a point where either they moved together or they would go their separate ways. They eventually worked the situation out. After a while the husband agreed to move to a larger town so his wife could launch her own career.

CHILDREN

If you are parents of a Low Progressive child, you will need to tell the child specifically what you want him to do and by when. Talk in terms of "doing things." Don't engage in the conversation of what he can't do, but what he can do. When he is feeling most defeated, talk about what he can do now and him for a time commitment. Make him responsible for that commitment.

FAMOUS FACES · HIGH PROGRESSIVE

Jesse Jackson, Ross Perot, Margaret Thatcher, and tennis player Monica Seles.

CHAPTER THIRTEEN:
USING WHAT WE'VE LEARNED

This final chapter will summarize what we've covered in the previous pages and show how features and traits can be put to use in a few areas of your life:

1. Children
2. Relationships
3. Careers
4. Sales
5. Trait Clusters

We'll also describe how people might behave when they share several traits – or possess what we call "clusters" of traits.

UNDERSTANDING CHILDREN

We need to be more aware of the strengths and challenges that children inherit. Face Reading gives you another tool that will help you immediately identify their innate abilities as well as the traits that tend to be more challenging. Teach children how to work positively with their traits.

A note to parents: listen to and support your child's dreams. It may not be your dream for her – it is her dream. Many people have shared with me that their parents did not approve of their chosen career. They tried the career suggested by their parents, but it never really gave them a deep satisfaction. It was merely a job. It wasn't until they were in their forties that they decided to make their dreams become a reality.

We are constantly reading about the horror stories of children at risk. If we can better understand their traits and talents while they are young, we may be able to help them avoid some of the difficulties they may go through later in life. Parents need this as much as their children, for parents have inherited their traits from their parents too.

They need to work on their own challenges, as well as understanding those of their partner and their children.

Here are some of the traits that we need to be aware of in children, along with some tips for parents.

PHYSICAL FEATURE	WHAT IT INDICATES
Fine hair (Sensitive)	Extremely sensitive; feelings are hurt very easily. Tip: If they run off into their room or suddenly burst into tears at a remark, find out what is going on.
Coarse hair (Less sensitive)	Love of the outdoors; may not appear to be as sensitive to others; tend to have louder voices and will enjoy loud music. Tip: If they are appearing insensitive towards others, explain to them how their actions are affecting people who are more sensitive.
Close-set eyes (Low tolerance)	Good with details; may focus on their problem to the point where it gets bigger than life. Tip: Check to see what is troubling them; help them to look at the reality of the situation.
Wide-set eyes (High tolerance)	May get easily distracted in school. Tip: Make sure they don't have too many things going on at once.
Narrow face (Builds confidence)	Hesitant about getting into new situations; for example, first day in a new school; making new friends; lack of self-esteem – especially if their peer group or family members are constantly putting them down. They will build their confidence through knowledge. Tip: If they are feeling hesitant about a test

or situation that is causing some worry, don't just brush it of with, "Oh you'll do fine don't worry." Find out what is causing the anxiety – it may be nothing much or it could be a big issue for them.

Wide face (High self-confidence)	Need to be challenged or they become easily bored; these are potential leaders. Tip: teach them to be sensitive to others; encourage them to help other children who are less sure of themselves.
Outer corner of eye lower than inner corner (The perfectionist)	Try so hard to do things perfectly and to please their parents. The parent(s) will have this trait. Tip: Praise them for what they have done. Encourage them to look for the good first in what others have done; be more sensitive to criticizing them for what was not done or the mistakes that were made. Look for the good first. It does not have to be perfect every time. Don't put your expectations on your child as you may set him up to fail or have a low opinion of himself.
Vertical forehead (Sequential thinker)	Teachers and parents need to know that the child is a step-by-step learner. Exams may be challenging for her. Tip: Encourage your child to ask questions if she has not fully understood what has been taught. When possible make sure she studies well in advance, this will take the panic out of exams or test taking. Praise her for what she knows. Don't rush her or surprise her with last-minute plans, as

	she likes to think it through first. She likes to know ahead of time what the plans are for that day.
Sloped forehead (Objective thinker)	Their minds work very quickly, they may not always get all the details. Tip: Encourage them think first before jumping to conclusions. Teach them to be patient with others who are slower.
More head behind ear (Backward balance)	There is a tendency to hold on to negative situations and experiences. Tip: Encourage them to let go of grudges – it's water under the bridge. Make sure you praise them. They may not ask for it, yet they want it.
More head in front of ear (Forward balance)	They love to be recognized and may create the recognition they need by doing or saying things that produce negative results. Tip: Give them the recognition and the praise for what they have done. Don't let them have to ask for the acknowledgement. Beat them to it or they may "act up" just to get the attention.
Long thumb (Intense feelings)	Both anger and emotions come quickly to the surface. Don't let them get away with their explosive anger; explain how that affects others around them. Suggest to them if they feel angry that they should go and find a place they can unwind.
Head wider at the back (Competitive)	The love of competing, winning is very important to them. Tip: Sign them up for a sport or activity where they can channel this competitive drive. Teach them to back off

	when they are overly aggressive to others. Ask them how would they like it if others behaved in such a way with them. Teach them to recognize and praise others for trying
Rounded ear	They will have a love of music. Encourage them to play a musical instrument or sign them up for singing lessons or join a children's choral group. Take them to the music store to find out how the instruments play and sound. Let them pick the one of choice. Rent the instrument first to see how they like it.
Trait cluster	Short legs, restless, wide-set eyes. May have a hard time concentrating. Tip: Get them to exercise. This could include sports, cycling, skateboarding, gymnastics, dancing or anything that helps to balance the energy.

RELATIONSHIPS

There are certain traits we look for in compatible relationships. This does not necessarily mean that there will be no challenges. But it increases the chances of the relationship being successful. We all have strengths and challenges; it's what we decide to do about them that will make the difference.

Many couples I have worked with said that if they had had a profile done earlier in their marriages, it would have helped smooth out the rough patches. Couples who are having challenges in their relationships tell me that the information gained during their consultations has completely turned their relationships around. Knowing their partner's traits has helped them gain a better understanding of each other. The relationship was important enough to invest the time needed to work on understanding their traits. One woman said her husband was now a gem to live with – no more erratic outbursts. For the first time in years, he took time out to be with his family.

PHYSICAL FEATURE	WHAT IT INDICATES
Similar width of face (Level of confidence)	If the man has a narrow face and the woman wide, she will tend to dominate the relationship. If the faces are similar in width, this would be a good balance.
Similar spacing of eyes (Level of tolerance)	If the woman has Low Tolerance and the man High Tolerance, this could be an issue because of the different reactions to situations in the moment. The wide-set-eyed person will see his partner as overreacting. The Low Tolerance individual will get extremely annoyed with the laid-back, do-it-later person. He/she wants it done NOW. The close-set-eyed person will come across as over reacting to situations. The wide-set-eyed individual will over-commit themselves and end up annoying their partner because they did not complete something on time.
Similar hair texture (Sensitivity)	This is one of the traits that is more challenging in relationships. If there is an opposite of this trait in the relationship, the coarse-haired person will see the fine-haired individual as overly sensitive. The fine-haired person will find his or her partner very rough or coarse and not at all sensitive to his or her needs. Their feelings get hurt very easily. The coarse-haired person needs to be more considerate to his/her partner's sensitivity. The fine-haired individual needs

to clear up any misunderstanding right away when his/her feelings are hurt.

Similar leg length (Prefers to sit or stand)	If you are long-legged, then your partner should be medium to long-legged. If you are short-legged, then your partner should be short to medium-legged. You will then enjoy similar activities. When there is a difference, explore activities that you can both enjoy.

THE CHALLENGES IN RELATIONSHIPS

Long ring finger (Risk-taker)	May take huge physical or financial risks. Loves to risk all.
Outer corner of eye lower than inner corner (The perfectionist)	Constantly seeing faults in what the other person does or doesn't do. The person with this trait may come across as being extremely critical of their partner. This trait is the number one cause of relationships ending. Look for the good first and keep criticism out of relationships. Remember to praise your children; don't criticize them, it can be devastating.
Exposed eyelids (Get to the point)	Constant interruptions, finishes off your sentences; this could annoy the other partner, who will feel they are not being heard or that what they say is unimportant.
Square forehead (Construction)	He or she may feel neglected when the partner is constantly working all day and all night. If this trait is seen in a woman, she will much prefer a career rather than stay at home. Make sure you keep a balance of work and play. Take time out to be with your partner and family.

Vertical forehead (Sequential thinker)	This person will appear to be slow to respond to questions. They are quickly irritated when they are running late for an appointment or catching a plane. They like to get there in plenty of time. If you have this trait, notice when your slow response is holding you back from taking action right away.
Sloped back forehead (Objective thinker)	They get very impatient at the slow response of the Sequential Thinker (vertical forehead). They like to do things at the last minute, which puts pressure on the Sequential Thinker. If you are an Objective Thinker and your partner is slow to respond, be patient.
Convex nose (Administrative)	These people like to be the boss; they are very aware of cost and look for the best price. They could get very annoyed when they see their partner being frivolous with their money. If spending is a problem with your partner, sit down together and plan a budget for the non-essentials.
Ski jump nose (Ministrative)	Money is not important, there's a tendency to spend their last penny. This could be a problem in a relationship especially when they don't balance the checkbook. Set aside some money that is just for spontaneous spending and don't go beyond that budget.
Head wider at the back (Competitive)	The competitive person will be frustrated if their partner is low competitive and low progressive. The competitive person will have great aspirations, while the non-competitive

person is happy with life just as it is. Use your competitiveness for yourself, don't pressure or nag your non-competitive partner.

CAREERS

Many people change their careers as many as seven times during their lifetime. Making a career decision poses a huge problem for many college students. They change their college major numerous times and often graduate still unsure about which direction to take. Many Stanford University graduate students have been referred to me because they are still lost in the career maze. Having changed their career goals so many times, they doubt their own judgment. The career consultation gave them the reassurance to move ahead. For students entering college or university, a career goal that is right will save them time and money.

Following are some traits to look for that reveal an individual's innate abilities. The trait by itself does not indicate that you have all of the qualities for the job profile; a complete Career Profile would be needed to see if there was a good match. To get the best results it is recommended that you contact a consultant near you. To find a person in your area please contact the e-mail address given at the end of the book. The Career and Personality Assessment Profile (CAPA Profile) can also be accurately assessed with photographs.

PHYSICAL FEATURE	WHAT IT INDICATES
Close-set eyes (Low tolerance)	Good with detail. Careers such as accounting, finance, health-related careers such as dental assistant or nutritionist, court reporting, teaching or counseling.
Convex nose (Administrative)	Finance, management, lawyer, project manager, investments.
Ski jump nose (Ministrative)	Nursing, customer service, volunteer work,

	sales (if competitive), preschool teacher (with close-set eyes), receptionist.
Inverted V (Design appreciation)	Architect, photographer, web designer, landscape architect, event eyebrow planner (with rounded eyebrows), computer designer, engineer, building contractor, interior designer.
Rounded eyebrow (Organizer)	Event organizer, flower arranger, engineer, resort manager (with Administration and Conservation) human resource manager, project manager (with Design and Conservation).
Oval forehead (The conserver)	Good at maintaining projects. Health-related fields such as dentist (with close-set eyes), chiropractor (with short to medium legs), counseling professional, teacher with close-set eyes, building contractor, hotel manager (with straight bridge or convex nose).
Square chin (To debate)	Mediation, arbitration, lawyer, environmental causes.
Flared eyebrows (Drama)	Acting, public speaking, sales training, teaching or any career that benefits from this natural flair for drama.
Head wider at the back (Competitive)	Sales and marketing, politics, police force, leaders of organizations and professional sports players.
Pronounced cheek bones (Adventurous)	Travel agent, tour guide, international marketing and sales (with Competitiveness and Restless).

The above notes are broad brush strokes. To get a more accurate Career Assessment you would need to either have a private consultation in person or, if you live too far away, from photographs.

SALES

As the old saying goes, "Nothing starts until something is sold." Another saying is that "We are all selling something" – trying to influence others for some reason or purpose. So, that being said, we are all salespeople on some level, whether we are "officially" labeled a salesperson or not. My comments here, however, will focus on the formal selling process.

Today, when there is so much customer competition, salespeople need all the tools they can lay their hands on. Being able to instantly recognize your customers' preferred buying styles will give you an added edge. It helps to avoid the "turn offs" from your potential customers. You can set up an immediate rapport with them. For example, you will definitely need to produce the evidence first for Skeptical individuals or you will lose them as your customers. Here are some of the key traits to look for.

PHYSICAL FEATURE	WHAT IT INDICATES
Convex nose	This is the bargain hunter. Asks.how much does it cost and can I get it for less?" Talk about the value of the service or product. If you have a special on this month, place an emphasis on the added value. Show them price comparisons so that he/she knows what a bargain they're getting.
Ski jump nose (Ministrative)	Talk about how the product will serve them; money is not as important unless they really have a tight budget. Chances are they will end up spending more than they intended, especially if their ears are laid back against their head. They will spend their last penny and then some.

Downturned nose (The skeptic)	"Prove it to me." Show these people the facts and all the information. They will want the proof first and be able to back it up with the relevant details.
Fine hair (Sensitive)	Talk about the quality of the product or service. If it's noisy where you are, move to a quieter place or they'll have a hard time listening to you.
Coarse hair (Less sensitive)	These people like things bigger and better. If you have a soft voice, speak up, use bigger gestures.
Narrow face (Build confidence)	Clear up any questions they may have and make sure they fully understand how to use the product. Talk about the support program that is offered should they need help once they have purchased the product. This is new for them, so there may be some uncertainty.
Vertical forehead (Sequential thinker)	Use a step-by-step approach; do not rush these people into buying anything or you'll loose them. Check that they fully understand the product or service. Keep checking in to see that it is clear so far. Give them some time to think it over. Be prepared to review the information again with them if necessary.
Exposed eyelids (Get to the point)	Don't get too detailed unless they need the information. Watch for the signals that they've understood and want to buy now. Just get to the point and don't use too much waffle.
Thin lips (Concise)	Be concise and to the point, don't go on and on or they'll get bored and turn off the conversation. Ask them open-ended questions.

Height of eyebrow (More selective)	If the eyebrows are high set, allow some time to get to know this person first. Do not come over as being too casual or move into their space to quickly. If you notice they are stepping away, it may indicate you are too close for their comfort. Give them time to make a decision. Or you could preface it by saying, "Do you need to give this some more thought?" Or, "Is there something you are not clear on yet?" If the eyebrow is low-set feel free to adopt a more casual and friendly approach.

TRAIT CLUSTERS

There are some traits which, when combined with others in what I call "clusters," can produce some interesting dynamics. Following are many examples:

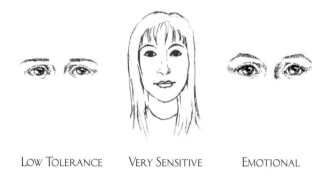

LOW TOLERANCE   VERY SENSITIVE   EMOTIONAL

1. When individuals have large irises (High Emotional Expression) and fine hair (Very Sensitive), the emotions can be more intense. People with this trait combination intensely feel other people's sadness even though they do not personally know the people involved in the tragedy. They are greatly moved by what is happening around them.

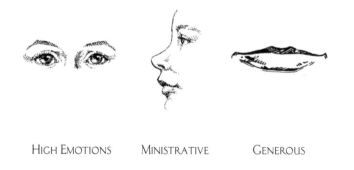

HIGH EMOTIONS   MINISTRATIVE   GENEROUS

2. The level of emotions plays an important role in the court-room in winning or loosing of a case, particularly if there is an

abuse or personal injury issue. Jurors will certainly be on the side of the victim. If they have a ski jump noses and full lower lips, the chances are that the money awarded will be greater than it would be from a jury of people with thin lips and convex nose.

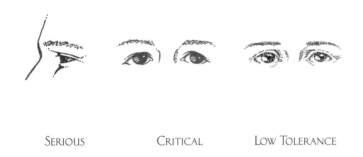

SERIOUS   CRITICAL   LOW TOLERANCE

3. A Serious individual can really take the fun out of life, particularly if a person with this trait also is Critical (outer corner of eyes lower than inner corner) and Low Tolerant (close-set eyes).

AFFABLE & AESTHETIC   ENJOYS PEOPLE   MAGNETISM

4. Women will be attracted to men who have the following traits: Low-set eyebrows (Affable), large irises (Magnetism) and flat eyebrows (Aesthetic) plus rounded forehead (enjoys being with people). People are immediately drawn to this profile. There's a magnetic pull. There is a great sense of passion and warmth in their faces. This can be very flattering and may explain why so many men with this

profile find it easy to meet women. There's an immediate feeling of being comfortable with them. This trait cluster is also seen in women and has the same effect. You will immediately feel drawn to them. Just remind yourself they are not necessarily making advances. They are just being their friendly selves.

LOW ANALYTICAL   HIGH TOLERANCE   OBJECTIVE THINKING   COMPETITIVE

5. Low Analytical, High Tolerance, Objective Thinking (sloped back forehead) and Competitive, these individuals will often leap before they look. They will often make a decision before all the information has been presented to them. They want to know what the benefits are rather than go into all the details.

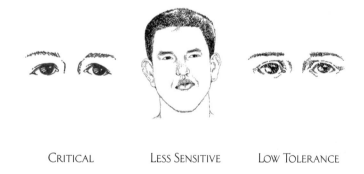

CRITICAL   LESS SENSITIVE   LOW TOLERANCE

6. People with a combination of Critical Perception, Less Sensitive and Low Tolerance will come across as being extremely critical without consideration for other people's feelings. Their

reaction will be shorter due to their low tolerance. These people can be very difficult to please. However, once aware of these traits, they can redirect them more effectively.

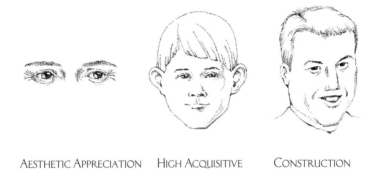

AESTHETIC APPRECIATION   HIGH ACQUISITIVE   CONSTRUCTION

7. Aesthetic Appreciation combined with High Acquisitive: these individuals may have a large art or photography collection. If they also have a square forehead, they will enjoy collecting books.

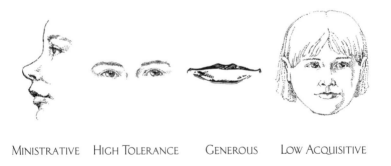

MINISTRATIVE   HIGH TOLERANCE   GENEROUS   LOW ACQUISITIVE

8. When individuals have a combination of Ministrative Nose with High Tolerance, High Generous and ears flat against the head (Low Acquisitive) they may find themselves spending their last penny and then some. This could be a person who is easily be taken advantage of due to their over-willingness to share what they have. This could be a problem in relationships. Money is often the cause of dispute in marriages; this trait combination could be the significant factor.

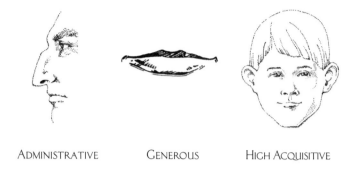

ADMINISTRATIVE   GENEROUS   HIGH ACQUISITIVE

9. High Administrative, High Generosity and High Acquisitive people make good fundraisers.

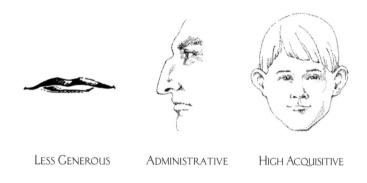

LESS GENEROUS   ADMINISTRATIVE   HIGH ACQUISITIVE

10. Thin lower lip, convex nose and High Acquisitive individuals hang on to their last penny. To others they will appear to be tight with their money. They will not spend more than they have to unless it is for themselves.

HIGH SELF-CONFIDENCE   ADMINISTRATIVE

11. Wide-faced and High Administrative people definitely like to be in charge. They will enjoy a career that is finance-related, although the traits do not guarantee success.

NOSE FOR NEWS   INFORMATION   LOVES TO TALK

12. If the Nose for News trait is combined with a flat forehead and medium to full upper lip, this trait combination indicates these people do well in the field of communication. Reading is possibly one of their favorite pastimes; they may be interested in pursuing a degree in the communications field.

OBJECTIVE   FORWARD   IMPATIENCE   LOW TOLERANCE
THINKER   BALANCE

13. When there is a cluster of Objective Thinking, Forward Balance Impatience and Low Tolerance, this person is likely to become quickly agitated. Careers for this combination could be accounting, law, investigation, medical science, quality control, inspection, IRS inspector or FBI agent.

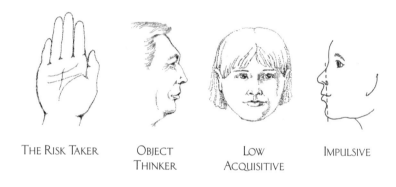

THE RISK TAKER   OBJECT   LOW   IMPULSIVE
               THINKER   ACQUISITIVE

14. Combine High Impulsiveness with Objective Thinking (sloped-back forehead) you now have a very impulsive decision-maker. Add the trait of Low Acquisitiveness (ears lay flat against their head) and Risk-Taker (long ring finger), you now have a formula for an impulsive gambler or someone who has a hard time saving money and is constantly getting into debt.

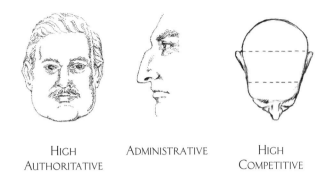

HIGH
AUTHORITATIVE

ADMINISTRATIVE

HIGH
COMPETITIVE

15. When there is a trait combination of High Authoritative and High Administrative, these people feel it is their "right" to lead. They blaze a trail for others to follow. They inspire others with their knowledge and courage. However, when something is not being handled right, they will take the task away and do it themselves, rather than explain how they want it to be done. If the above cluster is combined with High Competitive, this will be a very forceful person.

HIGH
PROGRESSIVE

HIGH
SELF-CONFIDENCE

HIGH
COMPETITIVE

HIGH
FORCEFUL

16. When High Progressive is combined with High Self-confidence (wide face), High Competitive (wider head at the back) and a forceful nature, these traits form a force to be reckoned with. If this also includes Low Analytical (eyelids visible), these individuals may come across as a moving force.

TAKES THINGS   SENSITIVE   AESTHETIC   DESIGNER
PERSONALLY

17. When the Taking Things Personally trait is combined with fine hair (Sensitive), straight eyebrows (Aesthetic Appreciation) plus an inverted v at the top of the eyebrow (Designer), a person may enjoy a career as a clothing designer, interior decorator, Web designer or any other design-related activity.

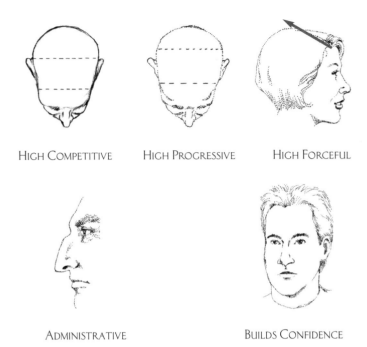

HIGH COMPETITIVE   HIGH PROGRESSIVE   HIGH FORCEFUL

ADMINISTRATIVE   BUILDS CONFIDENCE

18. If an individual is Competitive, Progressive, Forceful, Administrative and narrow-faced (learned Self-Confidence), this person may have self-doubts but to others they will appear to be very dynamic. Often friends or coworkers are amazed to learn that these people are intimidated by new challenges. It is the energy of individuals with this trait cluster that moves them into situations that are challenging. This energy is very magnetic; people around these individuals are inspired by it.

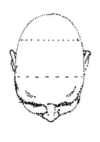 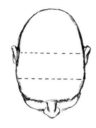 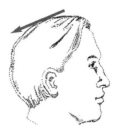

LOW PROGRESSIVE   LOW COMPETITIVE   LOW FORCEFUL

HIGH TOLERANCE   BACKWARD BALANCE

19. A trait combination of Low Progressive, Low-Competitive, Low Forceful, High Tolerance and Backward Balance will indicate these individuals are dreamers. They think more about doing something and may never take their ideas to fruition. If you have this trait cluster, or know of someone who has this more laid-back tendency, suggest they hire a coach. If that's not possible then create a short-term goal of two to three months. Make a short list of things to do each day.

CONCLUSION

Well, there you have it! My hope is that this book has helped shed some light on how each of our differences makes us not only unique individuals but also how we might better understand one another – and even get along better. No two people are exactly the same, but there are some ways we are similar.

As best-selling author Margaret J. Wheatley writes in her book, *Turning to One Another: Simple Conversations to Restore Hope to the Future*, "It isn't differences that divide us. It's our judgments about each other that do." Understanding our differences and appreciating them allows for better relationships, more enjoyable careers including healthier parenting and greater self-fulfillment.

GLOSSARY OF TRAITS

Acquisitive	The need to acquire possessions
Adventurous	Inclination towards change and excitement
Administrative	To administrate/oversee
Affable	Very friendly
Analytical	To analyze
Aesthetic appreciation	An appreciation harmony
Authoritative	Naturally authoritative
Automatic giving	Generous nature
Automatic resistance	To be resistant
Backward balance	Relate to what has happened in the past
Body balance	Built to sit or stand
Competitive	The love of competing with self or others
Conciseness	Brevity of expression
Conservation	To maintain and look after
Construction	Enjoys starting with new projects
Credulity	To be open to new ideas. Has a trusting nature
Critical	To be critical and notices the errors
Design appreciation	The appreciation of how something is designed
Discriminative	To be selective and more formal
Dry wit	Dry sense of humor. Can be sarcastic

Emotions	The depth of feelings express and felt
Forward balance	Think in terms of the future rather than historical
Growing trend	Interested in all aspects of growth
Hand dexterity	The ability to work with the hands
The idealist	High standards
Imagination	To imagine things in ones mind
Impulsive	To respond instinctively, verbally and physically
Innate self-confidence	Built in self-confidence
Magnetism	The magnetic sparkle in the eye
Ministrative	To spontaneously serve people
Mood swings	Changing from one mood to another
Music appreciation	A high appreciation of music
Objective thinking	The timing of the mental response to situations
Organizer	To organize
Pessimism	To be negative about life in general
Philosophical	Strong philosophical interests
Physical insulation	Sensitive to sound, taste, touch and feelings
Pioneer	To explore new concepts and new territory
Progressive	To take ideas forward
Pugnacity	To debate to fight for what you believe in
Restless	A need to be on the go

Seriousness	Takes the world on their shoulders
Sharpness	To investigate
Risk-taker	The enjoyment of high risks
Takes things personally	Sensitive to criticism
Talkative	A need to embellish conversation
Tenacious	To stick with something to the end
Tolerance	Timing of the emotional response to situations
Unconventional	An unconventional approach

INDEX OF FEATURES

ABOUT THE AUTHOR

Naomi Tickle is a world-renowned face reading expert and Certified Career Coach. She is the President of Face Language International and was responsible for developing the Career and Personality Assessment Profile (CAPA). She has designed a series of Face Reading card decks for personal/corporate coaching, teaching, sales, relationships, understanding children and jury selection. She leads workshops and lectures to audiences worldwide. People from all over the world attend her free monthly teleclasses (by phone). It is a great way to learn more about her work and be able to take that knowledge and use it right away.

Naomi has been a guest on BBC, CNN, NBC, Good Morning America and numerous radio interviews. She has been featured in *Cosmopolitan, Los Angeles Times, Sunday Times* and many other major magazines and newspapers.

Naomi has worked with hundreds of people who are in career transition, and couples who are going through rough spots in their relationships. She helps students decide on a college major, and works with people who are simply wanting to improve the quality of their own lives. As one client put it, "Naomi teaches us how to know ourselves and provides an incredible opportunity to create a powerful change in our lives."

Bibliography
Life By Design by Dr. Rick Kirschner and Dr. Rick Brinkman
Making Your Dreams Come True by Marcia Wider
Law of Attraction by Michael Losier
The Great Escape by Geoffrey Thompson
The Elephant and the Twig by Geoffrey Thompson
Essays on Physiognomy by John Caspar Lavater
Faces and Form Reading by M.O. Scanton

Services / Products and Contact Information

Lectures / Workshops

Naomi offers entertaining and informative Face Reading workshops and lectures throughout the United States, Australia and Europe. Workshop participants will leave with a working knowledge on how to use the information in their business and personal lives. A great tool for sales, teaching, coaching, meeting new clients for the first time or any situation where you are interacting with people on a daily basis.

If you would like a presentation or workshop at your conference or professional organization please see contact information below.

Career / Personality Assessment from photographs

Do you love your job?

Have you made several career changes but none of them really excited you?

Have you ever thought about doing something else, but are hesitant to try?

Are you going to college and not sure which courses to take?

The career and personality profile along with the coaching session will help you make those major decisions. The consultation can be in person or from a photograph.

Relationship Profiles

Discover which traits create the greatest challenges in the relationship and how best to work with them. Knowing each other's strengths and challenges avoids many of the rough spots that many couples experience. It saves hurt feelings and enriches the relationships for a lifetime.

GROUP CONSULTATIONS

These are available for companies or social groups. There's a minimum number of eight people per group consultation.

FACE READING CARD DECKS SERIES

This is a series of card decks that offer immediate access to information about the physical feature. A great tool for sales, meeting a new client, understanding your students, or simply finding out more about your friends and family. Each deck has a sketch on one side with at brief description of the trait on the back of the card.

THE MASTER DECK

This consists of 52 cards with a general description of the traits.

THE SALES DECK

This deck features the traits that relate to sales. A great tool that will help you to immediately identify your client's preferred buying style.

THE COACHING DECK

What are your client's strengths and challenges? What are the traits that keep your client from reaching his/her goals? Knowing the answers to these questions up front will empower the coaching process.

THE RELATIONSHIP DECK

Learn how to identify the traits that create the greatest challenges in your relationship. When both people in a relationship have a better understanding of each others traits, this will help to avoid the bumpy times in the relationship.

THE TEACHING DECK

Learning how to recognize key traits that will give you immediate insights to your students strengths, challenges and learning styles. It will help you to better understand your students and increase the quality time you spend with them.

Jury Selection

This card deck is a great reference guide for anyone who is involved with jury selection. The card deck will give you another tool that will help you during the jury selection and the trial process.

For further information or to order the card deck please contact Naomitickl@aol.com or call 1-877-THE FACE.

www.thefacereader.com

OBSERVATIONS

_____

_____

_____

_____

_____

_____

_____

_____

_____

_____

_____

_____

_____

_____

_____

_____

_____

_____

_____

_____

_____

_____

_____

_____

_____

_____

_____

_____

_____

_____

OBSERVATIONS